THE WITNESS

I Will Testify On God's Behalf

Holloway Gray

Artwork By: Mtgraphix Creative Group

Published By: M. Publications LLC

M.

M. PUBLICATIONS LLC

www.mpublications.com

Manufactured in the United States of America

Dedication

To my mother, Mildred Margaret Thornhill Gray, for the example she set. She showed me how to fight, how to press through challenges and how to live my fullest life.

Table of Contents

Table of Contents Cont'd

Part Two: Decades of Sickness

Foreword

The dynamics of spiritual warfare in this generation have been more intense and sophisticated than ever before. As the events of our time unravel and the levels of satanic attacks increase, there is a tremendous need for new dimensions of prayer and intercession to secure the victories of God's people.

New dimensions of prayer and intercession release stronger manifestations of spiritual gifts. I remember many years ago after ministering at MegaFest, the great conference hosted by Bishop T. D. Jakes, right behind the stage the Lord led me to pray for Holloway. The gifts of the Spirit began to move into operation and in the midst of prayer there were operations of the word of knowledge and prophecy regarding the life and family of this faithful servant of God.

I know that his experience with the Lord and the deliverances, which have been demonstrated in his life and the life of his family, some of which have been documented in this book, will be a great blessing to you and everyone under the sphere of your influence. The scriptures are packed with demonstrations of God's power to deliver and it is important for you to know that the same power is available to you today.

"Thou art my King, O God: command deliverances for Jacob. Through thee will we push down our enemies: through thy name will we tread them under that rise up against us."

Psalms 44:4-5

"Who delivered us from so great a death, and doth deliver: in whom we trust that he will yet deliver us; "

2 Corinthians 1:10

God is still commanding deliverances for His people and the life and testimony of Holloway Gray will bring you into new levels of understanding that will empower you to walk in new levels of dominion and authority over the powers of darkness.

It is my prayer that as you embark on this adventure of discovery you will receive the powerful revelation that is being communicated out of years of battle with the forces of darkness and the witness that victory is always the portion of God's people. This book is a mighty weapon that will lift you out of the pit of hopelessness and despair and cause you to see light at the end of the tunnel of any battle you are engaged in.

My eyes have seen the goodness of the Lord in the life of Holloway and it continues to assure me that prayer works. I encourage you to enjoy the testimony of what the power of the Most High God can do and I am confident that God who performed these miracles for Brother Holloway will do the same for you. This is your appointed season of miracles and divine interventions. Live long and prosper.

Archbishop Nicholas Duncan Williams

General Overseer, Action Chapel International

Introduction

Have you ever had a trial that lasted for years? Did you ever experience an unusually long season or extended time of testing? Are you a believer who is faithful to Christ, yet you find yourself walking through a very long valley of darkness? What does it mean to us to suffer as Christians and is there a root cause that can be unmasked and overturned? Whether you have experienced a dark season like this in the past, or you're traveling through a long valley right now...this book is for YOU.

This enlightening and encouraging book will help you master the spiritual weapons of warfare God has given you, discover the keys to breakthrough in every trial, and endure to the end to seize the victory in Christ. As God reveals to Holloway that there may be a reason behind this long, dark season, you are invited to come alongside him, not just as a reader - but as a witness. Despite negative reports from doctors, life-threatening surgeries, and demonic attacks on the lives of family members, Holloway experienced God's incredible deliverance, comfort and victory. After reading this testimony, by the grace and strength of Almighty GOD, you will walk with unshakeable faith in your Savior and Creator, Jesus Christ.

The Lord impressed on Holloway to carry this message of truth that will help liberate you. It is his deep desire to shout from the mountaintops the things that He whispered to him before, during and after these dark times of testing and demonic attacks. It was His voice that kept his faith from failing. It is my sincere belief that what Holloway has to share is wisdom, insight and a road map for you that can only be gained by traveling through the fire and coming forth as pure gold. God may have Holloway in a time of great peace right now, but there are many who are still in the fire. Holloway has written this book for those still enduring the heat.

While this book may read like a novel, it is filled with scriptural principles, tips on victorious living in Christ, encouragement for every person and a testimony that will show Holloway - and you - as an overcomer in Christ, ready for the battle ahead.

As his dear friend of 20+ years, I know that Holloway's testimony will ripple through the body of Christ as powerful words of triumph. Holloway has endured through a long season - tested in many ways, and trusting in Christ through every storm and negative report, even when God revealed the shocking reason behind it all. He is a mighty man of God who I deeply respect. His authenticity, transparency and truth will help liberate you and your loved ones. For every person who has walked through such a season, get ready for encouragement, get ready for answers, get ready for kingdom principles and get ready to experience brotherhood in Christ as you witness the trials of Holloway Gray.

In Him,

Pastor Paula White

I, Holloway Gray, do solemnly swear to tell the truth, the whole truth and nothing but the truth, so help me GOD.

Part One:

The Gray Family

Chapter ONE

CONTRACT WITH THE DEVIL

I remember it like it was yesterday, MegaFest 2004. This was the first year the conference was held in Atlanta, Georgia. All flights into Atlanta were filled to capacity. Hotel rooms were sold out months in advance. People had traveled from all over the country and the world to attend MegaFest.

That year MegaFest was held in the Georgia Dome. The inside of the Dome felt like a busy city. The place was packed. There was standing room only and everywhere you looked was a sea of people. Every hallway, every room, every corridor was filled with excited souls. With over 140,000 in attendance, every service seemed bigger than the one before. You could feel the excitement in the air; it was almost tangible. There was a sense of anticipation of what God would do.

I spent most of my time at the conference behind the scenes. I was the armor bearer for Bishop Jakes during this time. My job was to serve. I like to say it like this, to be an effective armor bearer is like being a ghost; you are seen but not seen all at the same time. I stood off to the side of the stage, behind the scenes, usually by the curtain. I like to think of it as the best seat in the house. I was able to serve and see first-hand the impact each speaker had on the audience.

People danced, shouted, cried, and worshiped...but most of all they were changed. People came in one way but left another. They came in broken and left renewed, rejuvenated and restored. The change wasn't only for the audience but I quickly realized it was for me too.

Saturday morning was the final session of the conference. My pastor, Bishop Jakes preached. The service was high and filled with a great anointing. Each point detailed and tailored to somehow fit each individual in the audience.

I was in my usual spot off to the side behind the stage, prepared to greet Bishop Jakes as he finished. With the final amen, the service was over. I escorted Bishop Jakes off the stage and to the green room. In a flurry of activity, our team greeted guests and began to transition to the next phase. The stage began to clear out. I continued to work when I was greeted by a familiar voice. I knew I recognized the voice. As soon as I turned around, I saw Archbishop Duncan Williams. I was familiar with his ministry. He preached at The Potter's House several times. Each time he preached it was impactful and powerful.

"I heard you need a kidney?"

Archbishop Duncan Williams asked.

"Yes sir," I replied, unsure of how he knew.

"Do you mind if I pray for you?"

"No sir. Thank you," I replied.

If you have ever heard Archbishop Duncan Williams speak, you know he has a distinct tone to his voice. It is sincere, powerful and deep. There is an authority that is audible and recognizable in his voice.

He stretched his hands forward and placed both of them on my chest and as he prayed for me, he called on the heavens and the anointing of God. I don't know if it was the strength in his voice or in his touch but I felt it. He specifically prayed for a kidney and healing in my body.

As he prayed, it felt like he brought heaven down to earth for me. Archbishop Duncan Williams seriously communicated with God on my behalf. It was not a long prayer but it was so impactful to me. When he was finished, there was a peaceful silence after.

With his amen, I knew that a connection had been made. Although I quickly accepted and received the prayer, I knew the rest was up to God. I felt His overwhelming peace and as the prayer settled in the air, I closed my eyes to remain in the moment.

Unfortunately, I could not hold onto the peace very long. The next statement he made shook me to my very core. Without any change in his demeanor or tone, he spoke words that I will never forget.

"Someone on your father's side of the family made a deal with the devil,"

I was at a loss for words. I could not respond and the peace I felt was instantly gone. In a split second my mind started to race.

"Did he just say deal with the devil?"

"The devil?"

"What deal?"

"Who made this deal?"

"On my father's side?"

"Was it...?"

"With the devil?"

"Did they?"

"How did they?"

"Why did they?"

"The devil?" I thought again.

Instantly I was mad at Archbishop Duncan Williams. How could he say that? Actually, I was not mad at him but mad at the word of knowledge that he gave. My emotions were all over the place. I was enraged, shocked, and confused. I felt my emotions boiling inside of me. I was in a collision of outlooks all at the same time. Although I was mad, somehow I managed not to say a word. I could not muster the nerve to respond.

If you know me, you know that I am rarely at a loss for words; it is outside of my personality. Typically, conversations and events do not shock me. However, that conversation did. The conversation and my respect for Archbishop Duncan Williams forced me to be quiet and reflective.

My mind continued to race as I tried to understand what I just heard. Any emotion you could think of, I experienced it. Every question you could think of, I thought it. Someone had to be the blame. Someone on my father's side made a contract with the devil, but why? What was so important that it was worth the sacrifice of your family? My mind continued to analyze the deal and the terms of the deal. I thought of each man in my family. For some reason, I only thought of the men. I didn't equate this word of knowledge with the women in my family. (Not that a woman is unable to make a deal with the devil, but in that moment it did not occur to me.) My father only had one sister and I knew it could not be her. It had to be a man in my family. To me, everything stands on the man's shoulders. Everything.

What if the deal was made before my father and his siblings were born? What if the deal was made before my grandparents were born? Who knows? I was so confused. I knew the only person who had the answer was God himself.

In the midst of my confusion, I could only cross out my father and his siblings. I could not believe any of the family members I knew could do something like this. I could not have imagined something of this magnitude. I thought of their lives and lifestyles; I knew they loved us and wouldn't have made this type of deal.

Next, I thought about my grandfather, Thomas Gray. I never knew him because he died before I was born. But, I thought about the possibility of him being the culprit. The more I thought about the person "who made the deal," the more I realized there was no value in it for me. These thoughts were a trick of the enemy. I realized I wasted valuable time. Who can trace the dead?

"I don't care who made the deal with the devil. I'm going to break the curse." I replied to Archbishop Duncan Williams.

"I'll pray for you," Archbishop Duncan Williams replied.

He knew I was in for a fight.

Sadly, I did not.

Encouragement

Have you ever heard something or had someone tell you something that stopped you in your tracks? What did you do? Were you able to listen or did you disregard the information?

Well, I did. As hard as it was to hear Archbishop Duncan Williams' words, I listened. In order to listen, I had to get a hold of my emotions. In that moment those words did not seem like help; however, later on they would prove to be very helpful.

Those words would be a reminder to me of who and what I was fighting against (the curse) and who and what I was fighting for (my family). I can look back at that moment and realize how God was showing me critical information that I would not know on my own. I did not realize it at the time but GOD was preparing me and providing protection for my family. GOD was offering me help I did not know I needed at the time.

God has always looked out for me. God has never forsaken me. God had been my help, even when I thought I didn't need any help. I am confident the same is true for you too.

GOD has always looked out for you. GOD has never forsaken you. GOD has been your help (even when you do not think you need it).

Even as you are reading this book, I believe God will use these words to provide, protect and help you. It is my sincere hope that somewhere in these stories and on these pages, you will hear His voice, listen to His instructions and take hold of understanding.

Take a moment to think about a similar situation or conversation in your own life.

1. Were you able to listen or did you instantly reject the message?
2. Was the conversation hurtful or helpful?
3. If so, why did it hurt you or how did it help you?
4. Is there a lesson that could be learned from the conversation?
5. If so, what is the lesson?
6. If not, what has stopped you from learning a lesson?
7. How have you implemented the lesson that you learned?

Notes:

_____
_____
_____
_____
_____
_____
_____
_____
_____
_____
_____
_____
_____
_____
_____
_____
_____
_____
_____
_____
_____
_____
_____
_____

Gray Family Tree

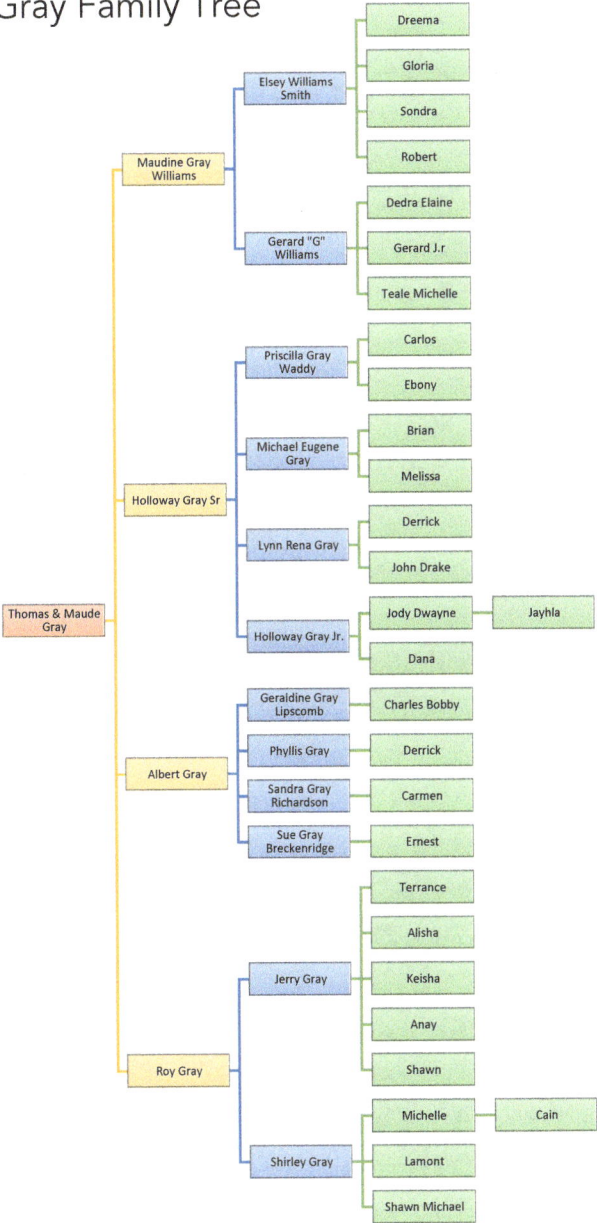

Thomas & Maude Gray

- **Maudine Gray Williams**
  - **Elsey Williams Smith**
    - Dreema
    - Gloria
    - Sondra
    - Robert
  - **Gerard "G" Williams**
    - Dedra Elaine
    - Gerard J.r
    - Teale Michelle
- **Holloway Gray Sr**
  - **Priscilla Gray Waddy**
    - Carlos
    - Ebony
  - **Michael Eugene Gray**
    - Brian
    - Melissa
  - **Lynn Rena Gray**
    - Derrick
    - John Drake
  - **Holloway Gray Jr.**
    - Jody Dwayne
      - Jayhla
    - Dana
- **Albert Gray**
  - **Geraldine Gray Lipscomb**
    - Charles Bobby
  - **Phyllis Gray**
    - Derrick
  - **Sandra Gray Richardson**
    - Carmen
  - **Sue Gray Breckenridge**
    - Ernest
- **Roy Gray**
  - **Jerry Gray**
    - Terrance
    - Alisha
    - Keisha
    - Anay
    - Shawn
  - **Shirley Gray**
    - Michelle
      - Cain
    - Lamont
    - Shawn Michael

Chapter TWO

WEVACO

"I'm gonna' break the curse," still echoed in my mind later that day. I didn't know what the curse was. And even in that instance, I didn't understand why I even called it a curse. All I knew was if the devil was involved, it had to be a curse. I was aware of the devil as my enemy and I knew anything he may have touched would be evil. If someone in my family bargained with him, there would be malevolence somewhere close. I knew I had to pay attention to the word of knowledge.

I continued to think about my family, person by person. My first thought was my father, Holloway Gray Sr. He worked in the coal fields of Wevaco, WV with his brothers, Roy and Albert long before I was even born.

Wevaco was country living. The air smelled musty, like a rough mixture of burnt wood and metal. It was so strong it stayed in your clothes for days even after you left town.

Like most of the men in my family, work in the coal mines was our tradition. The coal fields of Wevaco, West Virginia where my dad worked was different from Charleston, West Virginia where I grew up. Working in these areas was hard labor. A typical workday was twelve to fourteen hours, often two to three miles deep in those dark, damp, and cramped spaces. But my dad and my uncles didn't mind, they would do what was necessary to provide for their families, regardless of the challenges or dangers of the work.

I remember every day my dad would come home with jet black skin from being in those mines; the chemicals in the air would collect on the workers skin and clothes. And every night there was a special soap my dad had to use to remove the dust off of him.

My family told me that on one particular day while my dad was at work, years before I was even born, there was a bad mishap that changed him permanently. Dad left for the mines very early that day like he usually did. Hours into his workday, there was a terrible accident. Somehow a piece of slate fell off a ladder and hit him fiercely in the head. The impact of the slate broke the top of my dad's helmet and split his head wide open. Blood and panic was everywhere and he was immediately rushed to the hospital. On the way, while trying to stop the endless bleeding, the paramedics discovered that dad had some sort of heart condition as well. We would later find out that this was just a symptom of something much worse. When they arrived at the hospital, the doctors stitched up the jagged, seven-inch gash in his head immediately.

When I got old enough to notice my dad's scar, I often stared at it. I wanted to ask so many questions, but instead I just stayed quiet and I stayed in my place.

Dad never talked about the accident to me. Maybe it was because I was too young to understand? Or maybe it was because it too was painful to re-live. I knew it had to be bad though; it forced him to pull out of the mining industry all together.

Dad's health began to decline shortly after the accident. It started as an occasional cough, but progressively changed into a persistent nagging, deep one. In Charleston, many men had that same cough and unfortunately it was actually normal for us to hear.

As the sickness persisted, dad had lost a lot of weight. It was hard for us to see because naturally he was a big man, five feet ten inches and two hundred pounds. With his big broad shoulders and a large barrel chest caving in, all we could do was watch and listen as his cough worsened and this sickness ravaged his strong, tough body.

Dad never let on about the severity of his condition. I didn't even realize how sick he was until he was bedridden and forced to stay in the hospital.

The hospital room was quiet, almost too quiet. You could only hear the faint beep of machines in the air. Dad had to be hooked up to breathing machines, so our conversations were limited to my thoughts only. Dad could not speak or respond and I was too afraid to talk myself, so most times I just sat in the room.

I could not bear to watch as my dad deteriorated. It was the hardest thing to witness. Within 6 months he had turned into a man I hardly recognized. Instead of the usual welcoming, pleasant, big smile, dad rarely even smiled anymore. He was now quieter and often withdrawn. I think it was just too painful for him to do.

Towards the end of his battle with the sickness dad only weighed one hundred thirty-five pounds. His full, round, rich chocolate brown face turned thin, sullen and sunk-in. The vivid color of his skin faded from a beautiful vibrant hue to a dull, muted gray.

The disease had taken a toll on his body as well as his mind. It took a toll on our family and it took a toll on me too. He began to get very forgetful and often times he did not even recognize us. I took dad's memory loss the hardest because I was the baby and had never seen him this way. I had only seen him at his best. My father's condition left our family without a leader and it left me without a dad.

Dad never left the hospital. He died in 1974 at 58 years old. The cause of death was pneumonia and complications of black lung disease. Unfortunately many families in Wevaco, West Virginia, went through the same tragedy of death and loss as we did. Because black lung disease was so common, I never attributed his death to the curse, but now I know it was.

EULOGISTIC RITES

HOLLOWAY GRAY

My dad, Holloway Gray, Sr.

~Aunt Maudine Gray Williams~

Aunt Maudine was my favorite aunt. She was a sharp lady who loved to dress. Clothes, purses, shoes…Aunt Maudine had them all. Her accessories came in handy because she was always entertaining.

Aunt Maudine loved to cook. The family events at her house were full of the best food I ever had in my life. We had some of the best cooks in our family and at every event, each person brought their specialty.

Each family member would pile in the door with their clan and their best dishes. Within a short time, we had a full house. The music played in the background while the adults danced, played dominoes, cards, and pitched horseshoes. Uncle Roy always danced his way through the house and the food lines.

As kids, we ran around Aunt Maudines' house and ate until we were stuffed. As simple as it was, it was all we needed. Those family events were some of the best days of my life. As a kid, it seemed like those days would never end.

Aunt Maudine was a singer too; she had her own singing group called The Canaanites. On most weekends Aunt Maudine would entertain in different venues in Charleston, Virginia and in Ohio with her singing group. There were six ladies in the group altogether. Each woman brought a distinct voice and flavor to the songs they used to sing.

Aunt Maudine loved my dad; they were inseparable as kids. He was her big brother and she adored him so much she used to refer to him as "My Holloway." In fact, no one took dad's death harder than she did.

She was a social butterfly. She loved everyone and everyone loved her. She was the neighborhood helper-counselor-friend. If anyone in the community needed anything, they went to Aunt Maudine. She would help anybody, anywhere at any time. It didn't matter what you looked like or where you were from if you needed help Aunt Maudine was there. If someone passed away in the community, she was there.

She simply had a heart that seemed larger than life. You could feel the love and compassion when you stood next to her. That is what I loved about her.

With all the death she had seen in the community, it really shocked us on how hard Aunt Maudine took my father's death. The grief alone secretly ate at her body until she literally turned thin and frail.

Her friendly, social, playful and hospitable disposition turned into a quiet, solemn and nonexistent one. She just wasn't the same Aunt Maudine that we all knew and was used to. When my dad died, she grieved his death harder than what we could have ever imagined for a whole year. She passed away in 1975, one year later after my father. The doctors said she died from cancer, but we all knew she died from a very broken heart.

It broke my heart when I learned of my Aunt's death. I hadn't even fully wrapped my mind around my father's death well enough before I was faced with another tragic one.

Preparing for another funeral was hard. It was hard for the family and it was hard for me. It wasn't too long ago when we had to look into a casket with disbelief at our father, now it would be her.

The day of Aunt Maudine's funeral arrived. It was packed. The love she had shown throughout the community was evenly given right back to her.

The memories of our family gatherings were all I could hold onto while at her funeral. As I closed my eyes, I could see her full, round face and warm eyes like my dad. I squeezed my eyes tighter in hopes that I would see Aunt Maudine the way I remembered her, instead of the one I saw in the casket.

As we buried Aunt Maudine, I tried to block out any sound I was hearing to merely recall the beautiful echoes of her voice. I reminisced on a song she would hum and sing while in the kitchen as she cooked. It brought such peace to my soul. I knew if I could let her songs play in my ear, I could hold onto those melodies and let them ring in my heart so it would drown out the screams of the day.

Back in those days, I can't honestly say I knew how to process it all, you just dealt with it as best as you could.

Encouragement

Life can be hard. I know this to be true because my life has been hard. Life can be filled with death and tragedy. Unfortunately, there is no manual or manuscript for life. When something tragic happens, the Holy Bible is the book you turn to for answers.

Outside of the Holy Bible, I did not need another book. I am not suggesting that my story is in any way comparable to the Bible. Nor am I suggesting that my life is as significant. I am merely a man who used the Bible to make it through life.

I do not have all of the answers. I have not done everything right but I have made it through a lot of tragedy. Trust me, if I can make it through, you can too. I hope this book will be an encouragement to you and possibly a manual to help you through life.

Take a minute to answer these questions:

1. During crisis, what will you say?

2. How will you say it?

3. What will you do?

4. Will you make it through this?

Although these questions are simple, the decision you are making is not. Right now, I challenge you to make a decision to successfully walk through every tragedy in your life with GOD's Word, the Holy Bible.

Notes:

Chapter THREE

WHAT HAPPENS IN THIS HOUSE

The nurse came in every hour to check my vitals. Each time they entered the room, they would ask me a series of questions.

> *"Mr. Gray, can you tell me your name?*
>
> *Mr. Gray, do you know today's date?*
>
> *Mr. Gray, do you know why you are here?"* the nurse asked.

I was so sick and in so much pain I couldn't think clearly. Sometimes I couldn't even answer the questions. I didn't remember my name. I didn't know the date. I didn't know why I was there and instead of giving an answer, I just stared at the ceiling and then closed my eyes.

I couldn't help but think about my family again. This time, my thoughts moved to my cousins. As children, my first cousins and I played together as often as we could.

Growing up, our cousins were our closest friends. We played together at church, family functions, and Aunt Maudine's house. Our favorite games were kick-the-can and hide-and-seek. We would play outside until the streetlights came on. That was our cue to get back inside the house.

~ Gerard Williams "J" ~

Every night, he raced down the streets to our house. Gerard was the fastest out of all the cousins I had. He was a lot older than us though, he was about 12-15 years older than the rest of us. Gerard always won the races we played. He would run to the house, sit on the step and watch as the other children came in one by one after him.

Everyone wanted him to be on their team because he was just that fast. And whenever he played on a baseball team, Gerard was the first one chosen. He was a great pitcher; he would grab that ball and clinch it in his left hand like a boxer holding his gloves. He was a great player and all the children used to say he had a "mean left hand."

Gerard loved to draw and could do it very well. He used to draw cartoons and paint all the time. Sometimes they would have to pull him away from his art just to play. And had one of the most beautiful smiles that you have ever seen. He had a smile like my daddy. He kept a smile on his face all the time even when he was angry. He would be ready to knock your head off but still have a smile on his face.

Time had passed and I remember when Gerard gave his heart to the Lord. That boy was so on fire for God, his love for Him was so contagious that you couldn't help but be excited too. Gerard loved church so much and was faithful in attending every week. If you didn't attend church on Sunday, Gerard knew. His personal goal was to call people, encourage them to come to church and then shared the lesson.

He was a hard worker like all the other men in our family. He did what he needed to do to take care of his own. One day on the way home from work he wasn't feeling too well, so he stopped at the store to get some medicine. By the time he got home the pain became so terrific that he fainted. His wife Florence, we called her 'Sis', took him to the hospital for what they thought was maybe just a fainting spell. The doctors didn't want to assume so naturally they ran tests, which included an angiogram and blood work. When the results came back, everything was pretty normal, they said he was fine and he could even go back to work.

The next week came and he was getting ready to start his work-week. Sis and Gerard were watching TV while they were eating their breakfast. Gerard asked if she could put a quick hem in his pants for him before he went to work. Gladly, Sis walked up the stairs. Gerard grabbed the remote control and turned the sound up on the television but as he began to put it back down, he collapsed on the floor.

A few minutes later, Sis walked down stairs with the finished hemmed pants in her hand. By the time she got to the bottom of the steps, she stood there horrified by what she saw; her husband laid out on the floor.

"Gerrrrrraaaaaaaaaaaaaaaaaaaard" She screamed.

"Gerrrrrraaaaaaaaaaaaaaaaaaaard" She screamed again.

Sis ran to the spot where Gerard laid and tried CPR. She did her best trying to revive him. She didn't see it working, so she immediately called 911. When the emergency personnel arrived, they tried CPR as well, but they could not revive him. Sadly, Gerard died that day. The doctors said he had a heart attack although he was only 60 years old.

After he died, we found out that Gerard had a stroke five years earlier. We also learned that he battled with high blood pressure as well. No one knew Gerard had an underlying heart condition.

This information plagued me. It was information we should have known. If we had known, maybe there would have been something we could have done to help prevent it.

I tried a few times to open my eyes while lying in this hospital bed, but the medication had me feeling so delirious. I just squeezed them tighter together hoping I could squeeze the pain away.

I realized hours must have passed by, but for some reason, I just didn't care. This curse was plaguing me more than this pain. The more I kept processing this, the more this was all making sense. I began going down my list. All these cousins of mine, I never realized it before but they barely even made to 60 years old.

~ Elsey Williams Smith ~

Elsey Williams Smith was my Aunt Maudine's daughter, which made her my first cousin. Elsey was married to Leo Smith and had four children: Gloria, Dreema, Sondra and Bobby.

My favorite thing about Elsey was her cooking. I'm pretty sure she learned her great talent from her mom, Aunt Maudine. I don't whether Elsey was a great cook but the lemon meringue pies that she made for every family picnic convinced me that she was.

Elsey was as sweet as her lemon meringue pies. She took a lot from her mother. Even as a child she was just as carefree and fun as a party in a box. You could hear her light-hearted laughter around the house all the time.

Elsey's dream was to be a nurse. She always talked about how she would be the best nurse Charleston ever saw. So, she began her journey into the nursing field. She started taking classes and was on her way to living her dream.

One day, something happened to Elsey. She wasn't quite sure she even knew what was happening, but she felt different, very different. Her body began to do things that she couldn't control. It was unlike anything she had ever experienced before. Her body began to shake out of control. Once she came back to herself, she knew something was terribly wrong.

Elsey went to the doctor not knowing what to expect. They ran multiple tests to confirm what they already assumed from her symptoms, that she had an epileptic seizure. This experience was the first, but it wouldn't be the last time Elsey would have an episode. This instance would be the beginning of the rest of her life. This carefree, lighthearted Elsey we knew drastically changed when she was officially diagnosed with epilepsy. And her dreams of becoming a nurse were no longer attainable.

Epilepsy caused Elsey's body to betray her. She didn't laugh anymore. She wasn't carefree or fun. Sometimes the easiest task challenged Elsey because her body did not perform. Her mind was incredibly sharp and powerful, but her body was not. Epilepsy stole so much from her.

We did not know much about the illness before Elsey's diagnosis. However, we quickly learned the effects of it, her medications and the types she would have. I think our fear around the situation made it worse.

Elsey's seizures worsened as she got older. Elsey believed childbirth affected her condition all the more. After each child, she watched as the strength and frequency of her seizures changed drastically. At one point, the doctors had to put sand bags on her legs to even them out and help her walk.

Elsey's seizures continued to grow worse as time went on. They were now called Grand Mal seizures. This forced her to take even stronger medications. But the medications side effects gradually ate at Elsey's brain. It changed her personality so much, we just watched as Elsey grew more and more paranoid each day. We had to remind ourselves that "this behavior" was from the medication and that our Elsey was not like this. And this is what we told ourselves.

However, with each episode it became harder to distinguish between the medication and our Elsey. In our hearts, we knew that Elsey was as sweet as her pies but these drugs could make anyone bitter. Along with her temperament, the medicines had weakened her body as well.

Elsey had been sick for a long time. Her heart had begun to deteriorate from now what felt like a lifetime of being on those medications. She became very feeble and frail. It was hard for the family to see these drastic long-term effects of her condition and the medications that tried to support it. It literally caused Elsey's body to betray her, even to her last breath. One day, Elsey's body no longer had the strength to fight back. At 70, her heart gave out and she had a fatal stroke.

Her death took a toll on everyone, especially her kids. Shortly after Elsey's children buried her, tragedy struck their family again. This time it was her daughter Sondra.

To this day, the family does not know the exact cause of death. We knew she had a brain aneurysm and a heart attack. Sondra died at only 49 years old.

Elsey's children were happy kids. Her daughter Sondra was wonderful. She reminded me of my sister Rena and my cousin Sand. Sondra loved to play, laugh and always had a joke. We always saw her as the fun and feisty one.

~ Sue Gray Breckenridge ~

My Uncle Albert had four girls: Sue, Sandra "Sand", Geraldine & Phyllis. They were a close-knit family. The girls always stayed together and played together.

The Gray girls were typical teenage girls. Together with my sisters, they would giggle in the corner when boys walked by. They spent hours with their friends.

Even when they grew up, they lived close to their parents. Every Sunday they had family dinner together. They got married together, raised their children together and lived life together. We thought nothing could ever separate these sisters.

My cousin Sue was different than my sisters. Sue was meek-mannered and very quiet. Sue did not talk much at all; in fact, you would have to pull a conversation out of her. Our family joke was you would have to trick Sue into a conversation.

Sue was shy and introverted but very friendly. After Sue got to know you, she would open up a lot more. Although I knew this about her, I didn't always engage her in conversation when we got older like I should have. Maybe if I had inquired about her or just engaged her more, I would have known she was ill.

The last time I went to see the family, I saw Sue. I knew something had to be wrong. This time, there was a difference; she had more of a quiet demeanor. Her behavior had also lacked the energy that she used to have.

I shrugged off the thought with a list of excuses like, "Maybe she was tired", or "Age will do that to you" or "Everyone has an off day." You know, the normal list of excuses that we make instead of tackling the challenge and asking the necessary questions.

Back in those days, we just weren't raised to ask a lot of questions and or pry into things that may be classified "personal business" even if it were family. I am well aware now that maybe some of the things we may have been taught growing up, maybe it was beneficial for a certain generation. But had we not carried on that law we created, maybe we could have spared some lives or prevented certain events and circumstances from happening prematurely.

I could see the sickness all over Sue's face and in her eyes. And everything she did, it just didn't seem like her usual self. She used to bounce throughout the house to cleaning and cooking; instead, she sat there and did not move. But this time, it was different. I did not have to trick her into a conversation, she just freely spoke.

I left the family visit knowing that she wasn't okay, but I didn't think she was toward the end of her life. I didn't want to believe her quietness was a sign of an internal trouble. I wanted to believe she would be okay.

I came back home and a year later I remember receiving the call that Sue passed away from kidney failure. She was just 60 years young. Our family was concerned about how this would affect her sisters because they were so close; how could they cope with such a great loss?

~ *Sandra "Sand" Gray Richardson* ~

Sand was another first cousin of mine but she was the prankster of the family. She was always a beautiful girl. She had a lighter complexion and we would always tease and call her high yellow or red boned. My favorite thing about Sand was her sense of humor. She played practical jokes on everyone in the family. No one was safe and no one was exempt from Sand's jokes.

Sand would hide and scare us, switch the salt and pepper...anything to surprise us and make us laugh. Life with Sand was a constant joy. She continued to play jokes and pranks her whole life. She was so much fun.

As an adult, Sand moved to Detroit. Even when she moved to Detroit, we thought it was another prank. We waited months for the punch line; however the joke was on us.

Although Sand moved away, she remained close with her sisters and the entire family. Like all of Uncle Albert's daughters, Sand had one child, a daughter named Carmen.

As much as possible the sisters raised their children together and lived life together. From telephone calls to visits, the sisters and their families spent as much time together as possible.

On a normal day just like any other, we got a phone call. We were expecting the normal catch up and family update. In this instance, we did, but we heard the most disturbing and unexpected news; Sand had a massive heart attack and brain aneurysm and died suddenly. The news devastated all of us. We just couldn't believe it. This beautiful, healthy, and fun loving woman was now gone. Sand was only 62 years old. We were all still devastated from the loss of Sue, and there we were again, now burying Sand.

The grief affected the family and the Gray sisters differently. We wondered how the loss of two of the sisters impacted the others. However, it seemed as if the loss fused them even closer together.

Encouragement:

Speak Up

Where I grew up, our generations were taught not to get too personal. We were taught not to ask (people) too many questions. Do not be in anyone's business. We did not cross boundaries. We did not ask questions. We stayed in our place.

I grew up with the philosophy that "What is said in this house, stays in this house." We lived by that philosophy and we did not repeat home conversations. While we learned to be polite, unfortunately we also learned not to ask as many questions as we should. We learned that questions were not made to be asked nor rules made to be broken. We learned to keep to ourselves.

The issue with these rules or philosophies is that there could be an actual problem in the house. In our family, we have made a decision not to call things problems that are not problems. We believe life and death are in the power of our tongue. When we don't speak up, we allow the issue to persist. This issue could eventually turn into a problem. Ultimately, we choose to live with the problem when we don't speak up and address an issue. I understand there is a line of demarcation between being nosy and genuinely showing concern. More often than not, we err on the side of showing no concern.

Although those lessons were ingrained in me, I wish I would have asked questions and showed my concern for my cousins instead of following the rules. All I can do now is hope they knew how concerned I was even if I did not say it.

The lessons I hope you learn from my mistakes are to speak up. If you see something abnormal in your family, address it in love. Ephesians 4:15 reminds us "…Instead, speaking the truth in love, we grow to become in every respect the mature body of Him who is the head, that is, Christ."

We have held back and been quiet for far too long. We have allowed problems to persist because we have remained quiet. We have allowed curses to remain, because we have not challenged their existence. We have not done enough to show our love and concern, especially in our families. We should tackle the challenge, using our instinct by probing with more direct questions.

It's time to speak up. If we see something wrong in our families, say something. Address the curse.

So what about you...

1. Do (any of) these stories remind you of stories in your own family?

2. Have you been quiet about issues you have seen?

3. Have you vocalized your concern?

4. Was the conversation done in a spirit of love or accusation?

5. Was the family member able to receive what you said?

6. If not received well, have you tried to have the conversation again?

7. If you have not tried to have the conversation again, why not?

Notes:

Chapter Four

ALL BEFORE 30

Reliving these thoughts caused me to sit up in a panic. I instantly wanted to go home, so out of reaction, I tried to get out of my hospital bed. Then I immediately felt a sharp pain again.

"What is that?" I thought to myself. Maybe it was just the pinch of the needles that are piercing my wrists and my arms. The quick sting of that pain kindly interrupted my escape.

I watched as the nurse stuck me with another needle. I wanted to see if the needle prick was the sharp pain I continued to feel. I looked in order to brace myself for the pain. I twitched in response to what I felt, only to realize my movement did not ease the pain. The pain was so sharp it surprised me.

I closed my eyes again and hoped this agony would go away. But with each breath I took, the pain got worse until I realized that it wasn't from the needles. The constant, unbearable pain was from my memory.

I fought my own memory. I forced painful thoughts deeper into my mind. I desperately tried not to think back anymore. I tried to focus on the nurse or the machines or anything else in my hospital room besides my own thoughts. The harder I fought, the stronger the memories were. Unfortunately, this time, my mind went to an even darker place.

This curse was deep, it was multigenerational, and it didn't stop there.

~ Charles "Bobby" Lipscomb ~

My thoughts went to October 31st, Halloween night of 1991.
Charles "Bobby" Lipscomb was my first cousin Geraldine's
son. Bobby, as we called him, was an only child. He was
sweet, very friendly and a very social kid. Bobby was an
active boy. He played the trumpet in school and received
many awards for his achievements.

Halloween night Bobby was out with his friends and cousins.
They were just teenagers out trick or treating. They did not
have a care in the world. The boys ran from house to house
with their masks casually hung off their faces. It seemed like
the perfect night to hang out.

All of a sudden, Bobby and his friends heard a noise in the
dark. The noise spooked them, and in a split second, the
entire group ran as fast as they could. As soon as they
realized that someone in the group was missing the boys
stopped and slowly turned around to see who was missing.

In the shadows, they saw a figure in the middle of the street.
The boys ran over to the figure to see who or what it was. It
was Bobby. Bobby laid on the cold, dark street. Calling for
him to get up and noticing he wasn't moving, the boys ran to

the nearest house to call the ambulance. Their urgent screams and bangs on front doors startled the neighbors and the neighborhood.

Within minutes, a neighbor answered the door and called the ambulance. When the ambulance arrived, they confirmed the boy's horror. Bobby was dead. He had a massive heart attack. At only 17 years of age, Bobby was dead and his friends were shocked and devastated. Charles "Bobby" Lipscomb was the first grandson that died in our family.

I had no idea that Bobby's death was tied to the lineage of a curse. We did what a normal family would do. We consoled each other and came together as a family. It took years for us all to get through this tragedy. Little did we know, we would face hard times again.

~ Shawn Michael Gray ~

Shawn Michael Gray was my second cousin. At home, we called him Big Mike. Big Mike was a pleasant guy. He enjoyed life. He enjoyed his family and he never met a stranger.

Big Mike was a big boned guy who played football. He lived football and he loved football. Like many boys, Big Mike started his love of football as a child. He played from the midgets through to college and he was excellent at it.

Big Mike attended WV State University. He majored in criminal justice while there. He played defensive end and right end in both college and the semi-pro. He continued his football career through the semi-professional level, where he played for the West Virginia Lightning. In 1995, the West Virginia Lighting won the championship with a record of 15-1.

Big Mike worked to move his football career to the professional level. In 1996, he made the practice squad for the Philadelphia Eagles. Unfortunately, Big Mike had to come home because he couldn't pass the physical for some reason.

The news devastated Big Mike. The family couldn't see why not. He was big and strong and healthy. He had a very successful career so far, so how could this be? Him not passing the physical ended his career and his dreams. So many questions flooded our minds... "How could this have happened to him?"

After some time, Big Mike went back for a physical. His doctors discovered that he had untreated high blood pressure; this led to him having heart disease. The doctors called his condition an Athlete's Heart. We were able to find out theses details later on. Big Mike tried to fight through it as his health began to decline.

Unfortunately, he lost that fight. He died on February 11, 2002, from an enlarged heart. Big Mike was only 29 years old.

Our family suffered through his loss. It was eleven years since Bobby died. How could this have happened to our family again? It took years to get through Bobby's loss, now Mike's. I could not imagine the grief his parents felt. As I thought of my own family and my own children, I could not imagine this type of devastation.

~ Cain Edward Gray ~

Cain Edward Gray was the great grandson of Uncle Roy. Cain was born on January 22, 1995, in Charleston, West Virginia. His stepfather, a soldier in the United States Army, was stationed in Germany for several years. Although it was very different from West Virginia, Germany was home for Cain's family.

Cain was everybody's friend and could easily make himself at home. He was fun, outgoing and a daredevil of a boy. Cain had the most fun, which often landed him in the most trouble.

Like most boys his age, all Cain wanted to do was play. His favorite toys were his roller blades, his skateboard, and his bike. As often as his parents allowed him, Cain was outside on his wheels. He was all boy and he could not go fast enough.

Cain's favorite sport was football. His favorite player was Randy Moss, who he watched religiously. He was active in sports; he played midget league football on the Western Generals team. Although he loved it, he did not get to play much. Cain was too busy to go to practice, he had more important things to do like to socialize and clown around.

On November 26, 2003, we received a telephone call that once again crushed us severely. Cain Edward Gray was killed in a car accident. To date, he was the youngest member of the Gray family who passed away. Cain was only 8 years old.

It is still such a sensitive issue, as that loss was one of the hardest pills to swallow.

~ Jody Dwayne Gray ~

This third grandson is really hard for me to talk about. He is my father's grandson, my own son, Jody. I can't begin to explain how I felt when I held my son for the first time. The emotions that went through me were pure joy.

Jody Dwayne Gray, our son, was pleasant, kind, nice, intelligent and sneaky. Jody was the spitting image of me. He was a mini me. We had the same character. I was amazed to see him grow into a man and what a man he had become. He continued to make me and his mother proud. His decisions and character reflected the principals that we taught at home and his smile reflected the joy that was always in his heart.

In 2005, our only son, Jody was murdered. I discussed the details of this tragedy in my first book "Walking in the Shadow of Greatness."

The men who murdered our son were cowards. They had no idea how their actions devastated our family. They had no idea they were used by the devil. They had no idea they were part of the curse.

I can't explain how I felt. The emotions that went through me when I learned my son was murdered ranged the entire gamut. Our family almost broke when Charles died. We almost broke again when Michael died. We were heartbroken when Cain died but Jody's death...it was too much. My heart was inconsolable.

I didn't know if I had enough strength to survive his death. Most days it took all of the strength we had as we dragged our delirious bodies out of the bed. Some days, we did not leave our bed. We didn't have the strength to move.

I did not sleep either. Every time I closed my eyes, I saw Jody's face. I took sleeping pills just to get some moments of rest. I was numb. Sometimes I sang old hymns to bring us some solace and to help us sleep.

I was depressed.

Jody's death almost caused me to lose my mind. Honestly, I couldn't think straight at all. My thoughts went everywhere. There were times when I couldn't even put my words together to make a sentence, let alone make sense.

By the grace of GOD, I did not cross the line of demarcation. You know that fine line between sanity and insanity. Had I crossed the line into insanity, I don't believe I would have made it back. I know I would have been in a mental hospital. Somehow I did not lose my mind, although most days it was a close call.

One day in particular as I drove down the road, I reached my limit. I had finally put my thoughts together. I was beyond angry; I was enraged. I was confused; I was frustrated and I was nauseous all at the same time. I screamed at the top of my lungs at GOD. "Why didn't you tell me Jody would die? Let me trade places with him."

At that moment, I wanted to let go of the steering wheel. I wanted to watch as I let the car veer off the road. I could have smashed into a pole or even hit a tree. I didn't want to die but the thought of living without my son didn't make me want to go on.

The madder I got, the faster I drove. GOD said to me "Have you forgotten?" Instantly I thought back to high school, to the day I found out Denise was pregnant. Before she could get the words out, I asked her to have an abortion. I was too young to be a father.

I had no response to God. He was right, I had forgotten. GOD gave me Jody and for that, I needed to be grateful. Although the devil stole our son, I could still be grateful for the gift God gave to me and for the moments that we had with him.

When we lost our son, God gave me one word. LIVE. God didn't say anything else but LIVE. In order for GOD to tell me to live, I must have thought about death. My death. Somewhere in me was a thought, a passing thought to let go.

I wanted to let go of the steering wheel so bad. I wanted to let go of my thoughts. I wanted to let go and not fight. I wanted to give up. Thankfully, the word God gave me inspired me to LIVE.

I turned around and shared the word God gave me to my family. At the funeral and many days after, I reminded them of the word. LIVE. I said that I am just as confused as they were. I did not understand. I did not know why. All I knew was God was still God and all I said to them was, LIVE.

I believed this word, GOD's word to our family held us together. We made it through the funeral. We made it through the burial. We made it through the night, the next day and the day after that. We even made it through the next week.

It was a process. The healing did not happen overnight but we held onto each other and we held on to that one word. We held on to God's Word, the Holy Bible. It was a living, breathing, daily Word for us.

LIVE.

Encouragement

That is not normal. This is a curse.

I want to shine a light on generational curses. So many times we don't realize we are dealing with a generational curse. So many times, the issues we experience in our families seem normal…but it is a curse.

If everyone in your family died because of alcohol. That is not normal. That is a CURSE.

If all of the marriages in your family break up. That is not normal. That is a CURSE.

If everyone in your family struggles with poverty. That is not normal. That is a CURSE.

Take a close look at your family. What have you considered normal? Is it normal or is it a curse?

We have to identify the curse to fight it! In my family, one curse was premature death. I call it a curse because it violates one of the promises of GOD. In Psalm 91:16 GOD promised, "With long life I will satisfy him and show him my salvation." This means that we are promised long life.

Often times we let go of the promise. When we give up, we let go of it. If God promised us long life, I believe we should fight for it.

As you can see in my family, my father's generation died in their 60s. My siblings died in their 40s and 50s. My son and the grandsons all died before they turned 30. Cain, the great-grandson died at eight years old.

The curse in our family was literally cutting our lifespan in half. Within a generation, the Gray family members lost 30 years of life. The next generation was cut even further. If the curse was not stopped, I believe that the following generation might not have seen their fifth birthday.

That is not normal. That's not a normal lifespan. That was the devil. That was the curse.

So what about you?

Consider these questions as you think about your family:

1. What is the curse in your family?

2. Where has the devil stolen from you?

3. How has the devil stolen from you?

4. What will you do to stand against the curse?

Action Plan:

Make a list of what has been stolen and use this as your prayer list.

Notes:

Chapter FIVE

MY SIBLINGS

Lynn Rena, me, Priscilla and Mike

~Lynn Rena Gray~

My childhood best friend was my sister Lynn Rena. We affectionately called her Rena. Born on the Fourth of July, she was indeed a firecracker. She was loud and funny. Her personality sparkled like her smile. And we were inseparable.

Our favorite childhood games were jump rope, monopoly, hide and seek, and kick-the-can. Rena was better than me at most games, except kick-the-can. I could kick further than her, which was an accomplishment I was most proud of.

Rena was a tomboy with big brown eyes and a beautiful smile to match. I thought Rena could do anything. She could hold her own. She loved to play all the same things I did. I loved this about her.

"Hollowaaaaaaaaayyyy" she would call me.

Rena had a distinct voice, one you could hear in a crowded room. She was louder than the other girls but she was a leader. Rena always had a strong opinion and always gave it, even if you did not want to hear it.

As we got older, Rena played more with the girls and I went with my friends. We did not play the same games or have the same friends but we remained close. We had a connection that would not change with age or distance.

Later on, Rena moved to the west side of Charleston, so after work, I would stop over to see her. I would walk into the house, kiss her cheek and go straight to the refrigerator.

"What you got on the stove?"

I asked only if the refrigerator was empty. Rena always smiled and then let me sample whatever she had cooked on the stove and it was always good. Her food was so good that members of her community would often stop over for dinner.

We called Rena the "Block Mother" because she always had a house full of children. Rena was a single mother with two boys of her own, but on any given day there would be ten or fifteen boys in her house. She would feed them and let them hang out at her house. Anything to keep them off the streets and out of trouble, she would do.

Rena was Charleston's version of Martha Stewart. She was always washing clothes, baking, sewing or cooking something. Rena was always busy and rarely sat down to relax. Whatever was needed, Rena would do. She served the boys and many of the people in the community.

I was amazed at how my sister could raise and spoil two boys and at the same time feed half of the west side of Charleston, all on one income. Our family helped her with the boys as often as we could but she maintained her house like it was easy to do.

Rena always had a smile on her face and never complained. During a regular doctor's visit, the doctor told Rena that she had diabetes and hypertension. But that didn't stop her, Rena kept her same pace. It was as if nothing changed, at least for a while.

Over time, I watched as my sister's sickness progressed. It was a gradual decline. First, her diet had to change. All of the sweets and fried foods she loved to make had to be eliminated. Her activities did too. Our family had to limit the number of boys that were at her house to five instead of the normal ten or fifteen. Her house now felt different, almost empty.

Years went by, and on a visit back to WV, as usual, I stopped by Rena's house like I always did before to check on her. I was already living in Dallas by this time. I noticed the once vibrant, loud, outspoken woman I knew was now a quiet, soft-spoken woman. No longer active, Rena could only take a few steps at a time. She had to move around with a walker now; it was hard to see her this way.

I kissed her cheek, looked into her big eyes and did not see that sparkle anymore. Instead, her eyes were empty. The last time I saw that look was in the hospital with my father. His eyes looked empty the same way shortly before he died.

I blinked to fight the tears back before Rena could see them. I wanted to be brave for her. She had always been brave for me so the least I could do was the same for her.

We visited for hours this particular day. And after a few minutes, she seemed like the same Rena. We smiled, laughed and talked about everything. She seemed happy, even though diabetes had run rampant through her body. Somehow, Rena never complained.

I hugged her for the longest time before I left that day. I thought it would be a while before I saw her again because I had to travel to South Africa. I hated to leave her house but I knew I had to get back because we had MegaFest to attend. Neither of us knew, but that day would be the last time we ever spent together.

I went to South Africa with Bishop Jakes and The Potter's House ministry. Our trip was almost over so in our few moments of spare time, we strolled the city, walking, shopping and relaxing. All of a sudden my phone rang, it was my mother. She called to tell me that Rena was in the hospital on a respirator and we had to make a decision.

"A decision?" I quickly thought.

I paused because I knew what that meant. Our family had to make several "decisions" like this in the past. I got into a van so that I could speak privately with my mom. Within a few minutes, Bishop Jakes was in the van with me. He did not say a word just silently listened until I ended the call.

He could tell by the look on my face that the news was terrible. I started to tell him about Rena and then I fell apart. He told me not to worry about anything and that he would take care of everything. He planned to fly me back early to see Rena in the hospital.

The next day, before I could leave South Africa, I got the call that Rena had died. The doctors followed our decision to take her off of life support and she died shortly after. Rena was 44 years old at the time of her passing. She was the first sibling to pass away and the loss was unbearable for me. I could not imagine life without my sister and best friend.

I made it home in time to help the family with preparations for the funeral. It was bittersweet. Like Rena, her funeral was loud, vibrant and full of people. All of the boys that she took care of were now young men. All of them attended the funeral. I looked up to see rows and rows of these young men throughout the church.

All of the community that she so graciously served, had come that day to serve us. They cooked, cleaned and helped, just as Rena has done for them. It was such an extension of who she was and a perfect way to honor her.

Rena's death hurt me so deeply because she was my best friend. Seeing the way diabetes caused Rena to decline sparked tenacity in me that made me want to fight.

I had to fight for Rena and for myself. I did not realize how much Rena's death had taught me, but I would soon have to rely on those lessons.

~Michael Eugene Gray~

As a child, one of my closest friends was my brother, Michael Eugene. We called him Mike. He was four years older than me but we looked very similar, people always thought we were twins. We had to remind people which Gray son we were. As young boys, we used their confusion to our advantage and I will not confirm or deny any stories.

Like most brothers we were close, but Mike was more athletic than I was. It's funny, He played soccer, basketball and ran track. He was good at all of them, but he was particularly good at basketball. I tried to play with him, but I didn't stand a chance next to him on the field.

Like the Gray men, Mike had a warm and welcoming smile that drew you in; so naturally he never met a stranger. His smile was so convincing it disguised his temper. He was always very social and loved to laugh. He was a laid back, pleasant, and easy-going guy as long as you did not push his buttons.

The one person who could handle Mike's temper was my sister, Priscilla (or 'Cil as we affectionately called her). Priscilla was very calm under pressure. I think it is because she is the oldest of my siblings and she had the responsibility to be the overseer or babysitter for us on many occasions.

I remember one time in particular when 'Cil corrected me. Instead of sitting down and listen to her discipline me, I tried to get away. In my efforts to get away, I accidentally pushed her down the steps. Even as a child 'Cil maintained her composure; she didn't yell or fuss at me, she just kept her cool.

Priscilla has been a great example for me over the years of what composure looks like. Despite the situation, Priscilla was always calm. She was the best person to deliver any type of news.

I remembered, back in 2004, Priscilla called the house, as usual, to check in. Denise answered the phone and gave it to me,

"Hey 'Cil."

"Holloway."

"Hey, sis, how you doing?"

"Holloway, I have something to tell you."

At that moment, I could tell by her voice that something was wrong. I didn't know what it was, but I tried to brace myself for what she was about to say.

"Holloway, it's Michael."

"What about him? Cil, what? What about him?"

My heart began to beat fast; I didn't want to hear what the next thing could be. Each second in between words now felt like an eternity.

"Holloway. He had a massive heart attack. He didn't make it."

It seemed like my very own breath left my body. I couldn't believe what I was hearing. My nerves began to shake; my lips began to quiver. Nothing in my mind was comprehending anything she was saying. I just didn't want to believe it, but I needed to know. I needed to know what happened that instant.

"What? A heart attack?"

'Cil proceeded to let me know the details of Mike's heart condition. I had questions to ask but I was just too much in shock. I was speechless. For the life of me, I could not understand how Mike had a heart attack. He wasn't even old enough to be sick. I was sick long before Mike was. How could this happen?

Michael's heart attack was a pivotal event in my life. It is ironic how traumatic events can be etched in your memory. Denise and I sat in the living room as we tried to process the information from Priscilla.

I sat on the couch for almost an hour, still stunned by the news, when the phone rang again... For some reason, I reluctantly picked it up. I did not think I could take any more bad news. This time, it was Methodist Hospital on the other end.

"Is this Mr. Gray?" the nurse asked.

"Yes, it is," I replied.

"Mr. Gray, we have a kidney that is available for transplant for you."

The nurse continued to explain the transplant process.

"I appreciate your call but this isn't a good time. I have a family emergency. So, I will have to say no to the kidney."

"Mr. Gray, are you sure? People on the transplant list jump at the chance for this call. I will have the doctor call you back. Is this the best number to reach you?"

"Yes, it is.

"Thank you, Mr. Gray. Have a good night.

As soon as I hung up the phone, Denise had a barrage of questions.

"Who?

What?

Why?

Why not?

But Why not?"

I did not have all the answers. I only knew one thing, I had to be there for my brother and for my family. Their needs were more important than mine.

My doctor called me back within the hour. Just like the nurse and Denise, my doctor had a list of questions as well. Again, I did not have sufficient answers but I knew I needed to be there for my family. Towards the end of the call, the doctor understood my family's situation, my medical challenge, and my decision.

But while he understood, Denise, on the other hand, had a fit. She thought I would lose the kidney and miss the opportunity God had given me. I had to trust that God would honor my decision and allow me another kidney.

We made it back home to West Virginia in enough time to help my family with the funeral preparations and to be a support to our family. I needed to be there to hug his children, Brian and Melissa. I needed to be there to hold my mother's hand. I needed to be there to say goodbye to my brother.

I gathered my thoughts together while I laid in this hospital bed. The pain of these memories was never ending. I opened my eyes to see if the nurse was still in the room. No one was there. It was just me, my thoughts, my pain. I didn't realize how that word of knowledge would affect me so much.

Moment by moment, I realize this curse was more and more real. I knew my health wasn't in the best of shape, but I didn't know that I too could fall victim to this generational disease. Here's what I did know… I knew I wasn't going to let this curse get the best of me. I was going to get out of this hospital and I was going to be the tool used to get my family out of this mess. I was in for a fight, but I wasn't going down.

Encouragement

FIGHT!

The death of a loved one can be unbearable. I know our family has had more than our share of loss. From my dad, aunts, cousins, and siblings, each death was difficult and painful to deal with especially the death of my brother Mike and my sister Rena. Their deaths broke my heart.

Surely, you can see the lineage of the curse in my family. The curse of premature and sudden death plagued my family until we were made aware of it.

One way that I was able to move through their deaths was to learn a lesson from it. Learning a lesson made some sense of the tragedy. Don't get me wrong, the experience does not excuse the death or eliminate the pain. It is still painful. However, it helped me.

Death taught me many things. The major lesson I learned was to FIGHT. Through the pain, I developed a tenacity to fight for my family, fight for my health and ultimately fight for my own life. I want to encourage you to move past the difficulty and the pain you feel. Move into a place where you can learn the lesson(s) it needs to teach you.

Don't be afraid. Don't be timid. Don't stop. It's time to FIGHT!

Think about these questions:

1. Have you lost someone close to you?
2. Have you learned a lesson from their death?
3. What lesson(s) did their death teach you?
4. If you have not learned a lesson yet, what has stopped you?
5. If fear has stopped you from learning the lesson, how can you push past fear to learn from their death?

Notes:

Part Two:

Decades Of Sickness

Chapter SIX

HYPERTENSION & DIABETES

(1991-1995):

The cost of the curse

It was 1989 and I was finally clean. I used drugs for sixteen years and I can honestly say, I was a functional addict. I worked and provided for my family but I used drugs.

For once in my (adult) life I felt great and my body felt fine. Over and over I convinced myself that because I stopped using drugs, I was healthy. I didn't go to routine doctor's visits because I just didn't feel like it was necessary to since I felt fine. Now, on occasion, I would feel a little light headedness or had an upset stomach but that was normal for me.

By the spring of 1991, I finally decided to go to the doctor. I remember this like it just happened yesterday. "What could it hurt?" I thought. I still felt fine. I fully expected the doctor to confirm what I already knew...that I was perfectly fine. I walked into the office confidently. I greeted the staff and patiently waited for my name to be called.

"Mr. Gray?"

The nurse called my name and I quickly got up and followed her into a small room. As I sat in the chair, she asked me several questions and checked my blood pressure.

"Oooh," she said as the shock of my blood pressure reading hit her mind like a startling surprise.

I turned to look at her but she gathered her facial expression quickly, as to not give away her concern. The doctor came in the room as she was finished. Without a word, she pointed to the blood pressure value she had written down in my medical chart. The doctor had a stunned look in his face. Unfortunately, he was not as quick to disguise his shock or surprise as his nurse was. The doctor took my blood pressure again. The value he got matched the value in my chart. The Doctor said,

"Mr. Gray, your blood pressure is very high today. Are you having any symptoms of light-headedness, weakness, headaches or anything out of the ordinary?

"No Sir, every now and again I would feel a little light headed and or nauseous, but then it goes away, other than that, I always feel great."

My doctor shook his head…

"Well Mr. Gray, your readings are way too high. Your blood pressure is 180/100. This is in stroke range. At any moment, you can have a stroke or other heart-related complications because of your blood pressure. I want to take some blood work from you. I know your family history, but I'm not sure if this is an isolated incident or if this is normal."

They drew my blood and I went home. Two days later I received a call from the doctor's office confirming that I have Hypertension and they have to put me on medication right away.

I didn't expect that news, but I wasn't too surprised… after all, the doctor said it could have been hereditary. I was asked to return in two weeks. Although I felt fine, I was worse than before. The doctors called my condition Malignant Hypertension. They started me on different types of blood pressure medication to see what would work best. My blood pressure would spike to 200/100 often. My body was in constant pain, but I didn't realize it.

Maybe it was the years of drug abuse, but I felt normal. Each time I went to my doctors' appointments they looked at me as if any moment my head would explode. To them, I was a time bomb just waiting to explode.

Reluctantly, I agreed to get on medication. Their concern of my constant stroke level readings made me antsy. I felt defeated. I felt like I was punished with the diagnosis because I went to the appointment. Although I was still sick before the visit, somehow mentally, the diagnosis made it real.

It took the doctor about a month to get me on the correct dosage and number of medications. My blood pressure was so high and had been uncontrolled for so long, that it was difficult to get it under control. The medication made me groggy, sleepy and sometimes even irritable.

At first, my medication was prescribed for once a day. That quickly changed to two times per day. This finally got my blood pressure into a normal range. Because of the years of my prior drug abuse, my body's tolerance for medication was extremely high and I simply could not feel the effects of it.

To be honest, I did not take my medication every day, in fact, I didn't take it seriously so I didn't take it as I should have. I hated how tired it made me feel. I had to work and provide for my family. I didn't have time to slow down and I certainly didn't have time to sleep.

That mindset was me covering up my true feelings. I fell into depression over this, really bad, but I was able to mask it with work. My wife and kids didn't even notice. I just went through the motions for the next six months, but inside I was dying. But truly, what was dying was my pride.

To be honest, I thought I was invincible. I would whine and complain and ask "How could this happen to me? I'm not old enough to be on this type of medication. I'm Holloway. This doesn't happen to me." I was always strong, active and healthy, even with years of drugs abuse, so my pride was being harshly challenged.

I decided that I needed to pay closer attention to my body. When I think back, we didn't eat very healthy back then either. Clearly I missed the symptoms of hypertension. I wanted to make sure I was fine and healthy from here on out.

By the spring of 1992, I noticed another change in my body. I was thirsty all the time, really thirsty. I could not get enough to drink. However, I did drink a lot of sodas and juices. No matter how much I drank, nothing quenched my thirst. Then I noticed another change in my body. I urinated all the time. At first, I thought it was because I drank so much. However the number of times I went to the bathroom was not equivalent and I just couldn't figure it out

Next, I began to lose weight. Although I ate frequently, I continued to lose weight. I lost about 15lbs the first month, then another 15lbs the next month; I did not know what was wrong with me. That was a lot of weight loss and it scared me. It scared me to the point that I didn't even want to go to the doctor to see what was wrong. The only logical thing I thought to do was eat more to put the weight back on.

By this time, the devil plagued my mind with thoughts of death. He started to tell me I had AIDS. The questions and thoughts of whether I had the virus from years of drug abuse continued to torment my mind. I started to rationalize my drug use and reckless behavior. I wondered whether this was my punishment for my previous lifestyle.

I couldn't sleep at night and my clothes didn't fit me anymore. They were falling off of me and I was ashamed of how I looked and saw myself. I was overly nervous and just scared. So nervous I kept hearing all these voices in my head telling me, "You don't know what you have." I was doing my best trying to hide my shame and embarrassment. Denise was so concerned, but I just kept telling her I was okay. I wasn't and I knew it. I knew I had to get to the doctor regardless of how scared it was.

After about the 3rd month, I went to the physician. I went out of fear but I went. I was afraid for my life and needed reassurance. I walked into the doctor's office slowly. I patted my foot on the floor as I waited for him to come into the office. I answered all of the questions I was asked. Each time, I looked in the doctor's face for reassurance, but he did not respond. He only asked more questions.

He left the office for what felt like hours. As I sat there the thoughts came back to me about the life threatening conditions I may have.

Was it AIDS?

Was it Cancer?

Was it some rare disorder that had no cure and high mortality rate?

Was I going to die?

Thankfully the doctor opened the door before my mind could go to a deeper and darker place.

"Mr. Gray, thank you for your patience. I could tell almost immediately from the symptoms you described to me and what you were experiencing, that you had diabetes, but I wanted to run some quick tests to confirm and see to what extent. Unfortunately Mr. Gray, theses tests did come back positive, you have Type II Diabetes."

"Diabetes?" I said with quick relief; that was much better than what I thought.

But that positive moment didn't last too long. Although the diagnosis was not a death sentence, it felt like one. The look on the doctors' face made me question my health again. Hypertension coupled with diabetes was a bad combination and I knew it. The doctor prescribed me medication right away.

As I took my pills, I wondered why me. What did I do to deserve this? I was a big, strong man but this diagnosis hit me hard. Each time I took a pill, I realized I was not invincible. Each time I took a pill, I wondered if it would cause me to relapse into drug use.

Mentally, I fought the diagnosis and the medication on a daily basis. I wanted to be well. I felt fine but the diagnosis was a reminder that my mind had played tricks on me.

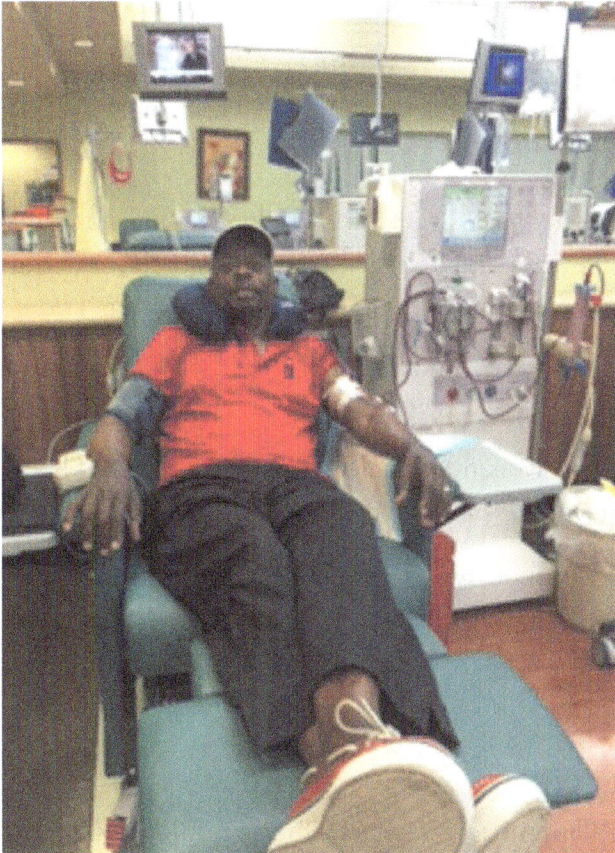

6am dialysis

Encouragement

MIRACLE

I know that I am a walking miracle. I am alive and that is a miracle. I am able to walk. That is a miracle. I am not addicted to drugs anymore. That is a miracle. I do not look like what I have been through.

You are a walking miracle as well. You may not know it, your life may not look miraculous right now but it is.

You may think diabetes and hypertension are not death sentences, but you will shortly see my battle was far from over.

With all of the loss my family had endured, I did not lose my mind. The word of God has sustained me. It has become what I depend on every day. I totally believe and rely on the word of God. Even in the midst of dilemmas and tragedy, stay focused on the word of God.

I know that the same word that sustained me will sustain you. Try it. Take hold of the promises of God and trust His Word that He will do it.

Notes:

Chapter SEVEN

EYE FOR AN EYE
1995-2000

I stared at the walls for minutes at a time as I tried to identify what I saw. There was a greyish-cloudy spot on the ceiling that was not there yesterday. Did something happen? I thought. Was it water damage? Was it mold? What in the world was it?

As I tried to figure out the reason for the spot on the ceiling, I started to look at the rest of the walls. I stared for a minute and then it happened again; I saw another spot. Again, I thought is this water damage from the ceiling? Where did this come from? I kept racking my brain; maybe I need to check the entire house?

So, I walked throughout and found spots that I had not seen before. I had Denise check the areas as well but strangely enough, she did not see the spots that I saw. Clearly, she hadn't paid attention to the areas that I pointed out.

Well, was I going blind? I thought I was going blind or maybe just going crazy. Each day the spots seemed bigger and took up more of my vision. I hated to close my eyes (or hated to sleep), for fear of what I would not be able to see when I opened them.

The next day I walked through the house, only to find the spots had disappeared. Maybe Denise was right, or maybe something else was wrong.

Reluctantly I scheduled an appointment with my eye doctor. Days later, I walked into this office slightly concerned because the spots had come back. I explained the situation to him and I watched as his facial expression changed. It reminded me of the look I saw in my other doctor's face when they diagnosed me with malignant hypertension.

He quickly determined that my vision was poor and required surgery. He said this vision impairment was a direct result of the side effects of my diabetes. My sugar levels would reach as high as the 300's sometimes.

In 2001, I began a series of eye surgeries. The surgeries were to repair a detached retina and for glaucoma. I had five surgeries within a year. Each procedure was approximately three weeks apart.

During each surgery, the doctors would treat my eyes with a laser. First, he would numb my eye by taking a large needle and injecting the Lidocaine into it. I could still see but could not feel any pain. I could, however, feel pressure and each laser application was filled with a good deal of pressure.

Now, there was only so much laser applications I could take directly in the eye to stop the bleeding. These laser doses only lasted about 10 minutes at a time. I had the same procedure done on both eyes and the doctors would perform the procedure biweekly. I had multiple surgeries during a five-week period. The total procedure took approximately four months for both eyes to be treated.

That's another reason why I worked all the time. Work kept me up and kept my eyes opened. I thought if I didn't close them, I couldn't lose my vision.

There is a distinct panic that sits in the pit of your stomach when you are being prepared for eye surgery. The fear forces you to look at every painstaking detail in the event of a problem. I tried to memorize what every color looked like. I tried to soak in the day's sunrise and sunset. I tried to close my eyes and see things as vividly as I saw them when my eyes were opened, but unfortunately, I failed every time, which only intensified the panic.

I could hardly breathe as the doctors prepared me for surgery. I panicked. I fought the medication and I fought for my last few minutes of sight. One nurse held my hand while another spoke to me in the most calming tone I ever heard. The nurses repeatedly reminded me to keep my head still. I wish the doctors could have put me to sleep.

After surgery, I had a patch over one eye. I grabbed at it often to make sure it was real and that I was not blind. I sat with the same panic as I did before the surgery, with this fear in the pit of my stomach. It was only by the grace of God that I did not lose my vision or my mind.

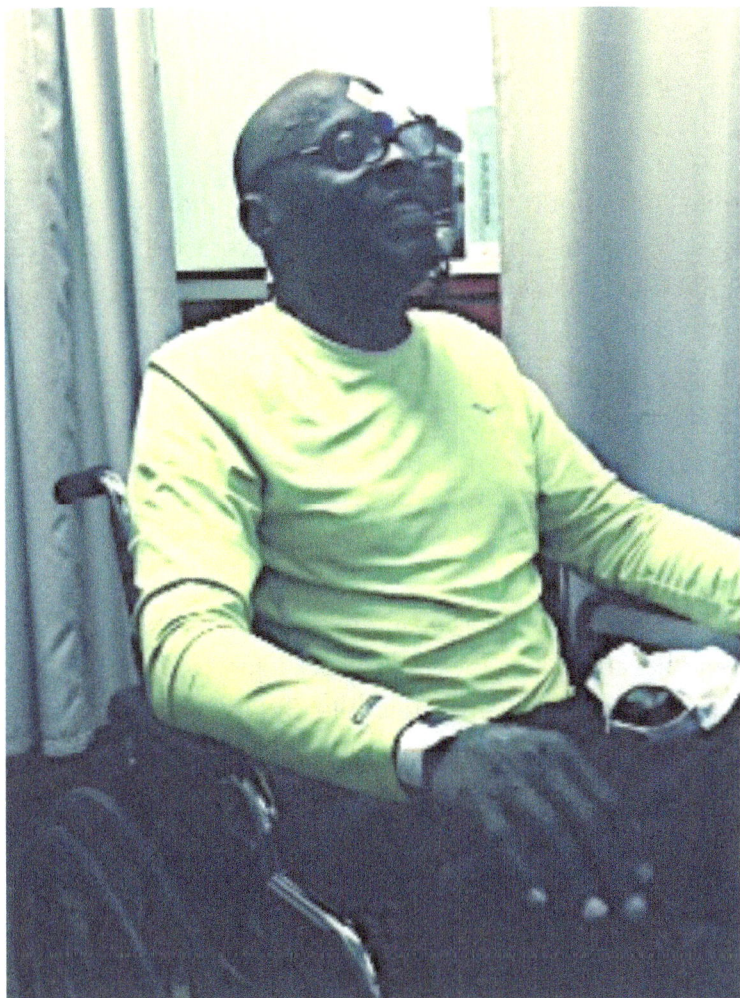

My left eye patched after surgery to repair retinal   detachment.

Encouragement

When I talk about "sickness", I don't mean the flu or a cold. I was sick unto death. I almost died on several occasions. This (battle with sickness) is a part of life and you have to live it or it will swallow you up. Although you do not know what life will throw at you, you have to face it and live anyway. I would not want anyone else to go through what I went through in the past twenty years. I would not wish this on my worst enemy.

Some days the pain was so intense I could not bear it. I would have to take a lot of medication just to be able to function; that pain was unbearable. But in the midst of it, I had to make a decision. I quickly decided I would have to stand in the gap and break the lineage of the curse in my family. I had no idea that I was in for the fight of my life. I had no idea what this fight would cost me, but I knew I had to fight.

One way to fight is to keep your emotions under control. Often times when tragedy hits us, our emotions get the best of us. These emotions can push us or drive us in a direction we don't want to go. Our emotions can direct us to the opposite side of our faith. I have learned to keep my emotions at bay. So, therefore, I am not a person who faints or falls out under pressure and I don't freak out either.

This is not to condemn you if you do freak out under pressure. Just realize that you have to keep it together. Remain focused on the Word of God so you can speak your faith. Faith is the only thing that will change the situation.

Don't let the heat of the situation or tragedy cause you to lose focus. Look above your current circumstances. Look to GOD. Even in the middle of the battle, stay focused and fixed on Gods Word. It will sustain you. (It sustained me even in the hardest of battles and I made it through).

- Keep your emotions at bay.

- Stay focused on GOD.

- Stay focused on God's Word.

- God's Word will see you through.

The eye surgeries taught me what the Bible means as it gives the definition of faith. In Hebrews 11:1 "Now faith is the substance of things hoped for, the evidence of things not seen."

I had to rely on what I believed (healing) and not what I could see (black spots and holes). I had to know my vision would be restored when all of the symptoms pointed to vision loss or blindness.

Allow me encourage you to believe. Hold on to your faith. Hold on to what you cannot see.

Notes:

Chapter EIGHT

KIDNEYS

Archbishop Duncan Williams' prayers worked. The same day, Methodist Hospital called me and confirmed there were two kidneys available for transplant. The nurse continued to tell me about the kidneys and that I was not the first transplant candidate but the second. In the event the first candidate was not eligible, I would receive the kidneys.

We flew from MegaFest in Atlanta directly into Dallas. I had arranged a car to pick us up from the airport and take us to Methodist Hospital. On the car ride over, I wrestled with the thought of not getting the transplant. I had decided before we walked into the hospital that whatever the outcome was, we would thank the Lord.

We arrived at the hospital to find the first candidate was already being tested. As we waited, Denise and I began to pray for them. We asked God to bless her and keep her healthy. We trusted God and believed He would provide for both the first candidate and myself.

The doctors slowly walked down the hall toward me. I could not read their faces, although I tried. The disappointment I saw on their faces told me I would not get the kidneys. But I was wrong. The doctor walked passed me to the first candidate's family. He briefly consoled the family before he looked in our direction.

The doctor immediately walked over to Denise and I. They explained that the first candidate was not eligible for the transplant. I didn't know whether to be happy for myself or disappointed for them. I was torn. I listened as the doctor explained that I would need to have a battery of test done and the test would determine whether or not I was healthy enough to have the surgery.

I said a silent prayer as we left the waiting room and walked back into my hospital room.

"Dear GOD, please help me." I whispered.

As soon as the nurses started my tests, I could tell God heard me. Hour after hour went by as I waited for the results, but when they came, they came with a flurry of activity. I received one result and then another. Quickly doctors and nurses poured into my room. In a matter of moments, I went from getting results to getting prepared for surgery.

I was not as nervous for the transplant as I was for the eye surgeries. Honestly, I didn't have time to be nervous. I was sleep before I could even process the next thought.

I was amazed how the transplant team moved so quickly and seamlessly. This was a regular day for them but for me it was an answer to prayer and a life-changing event.

The surgery took about four hours. I was surprised that I was not groggy when I woke up. It felt like I took a much-needed nap. I was rested but incredibly sore. I could hardly move. I had a large vertical incision from my chest to my stomach. It hurt to breathe. It hurt to smile. It hurt to lay on the bed. I wanted to get up and move but the pain was so intense, I had to listen to the nurses' orders.

As I laid on the bed, all I could do was think. I didn't have many other options. So I began to process what just happened and what my next steps would be. First, revisit that prayer again; then, receiving these brand new kidneys. Next, I thought about the progress I would have to make to get up, get home and go back to work. Don't get me wrong, I was so thankful to have received the kidney transplant because I knew this would allow me to enjoy life and I would have my freedom again.

The road to recovery was harder than I thought. Although it was unrealistic, I wanted to be home by the end of the week. I spent several weeks in the hospital as my body tried to adjust to the new organs. I lost about 60 pounds during the transplant process. I thought I would be healed in about six months or so, but it took closer to eighteen months to get back to normal.

Before I was discharged, the transplant team explained my healing process and my medication. I would have to take anti-rejection medicine for the rest of my life. As I listened to their instructions, I felt the disappointment grow in my chest.

It sounds crazy to be disappointed after you successfully made it through this type of surgery, but I was. Surgery is traumatic and has risks, so I knew I should be happy, but I wasn't. I wrestled with the thought of being on a lot of medication again. It felt like taking drugs. The idea of struggling with a drug addiction again depressed me.

As a man, it's hard to admit when you lose control. But somewhere in the sickness and the mental battle against drug addiction, I lost control. I couldn't pull myself out of the mental pit I fell into. I experienced depression…levels of depression so deep I wasn't sure I could escape.

I watched family and friends surround me with support and prayer. It helped most days but sometimes it seemed like nothing helped. There were some things I had to battle with by myself. And this was a fight.

There were times I could not get out of bed.

There were times I did not eat.

There were times I did not sleep.

There were times I did not bathe or shave.

There were times I did not want to have relations with my wife.

I was so enthralled with the sickness I could not focus. By this time, I had lived through sickness after sickness for more than a decade. As much as it affected my body, it also affected my mind. I began to see myself differently. Every day when I looked in the mirror, I saw this frail, weak looking reflection stare back at me. I didn't resemble the big, strong stud of a man I thought I was. I felt like the mirror constantly betrayed me. It was just one daily reminder that the sickness was winning.

I was losing this battle and needed to do something quick. My mind flashed to thoughts of my dad, my aunts and my sister. I remember the frail look of their bodies and the sunken look of their faces. But the look of defeat in their eyes before they died is what is embedded in me.

I was depressed. I lost control and became just flat out mean. I lashed out on my wife and was just so mean to her at times. I was embarrassed over the things I said to her, but I couldn't help myself. I didn't mean everything I said, but I said them and that was wrong. She did nothing but nurse me and love me. Unfortunately, she was the only person I could reach, so I took my frustrations out on her.

Depression is terrible. You cannot play with it. If you are unaware, depression can kill you. Depression will cause you to spiral down to a point where you cannot get out. I know unquestionably that depression is a trick of the devil.

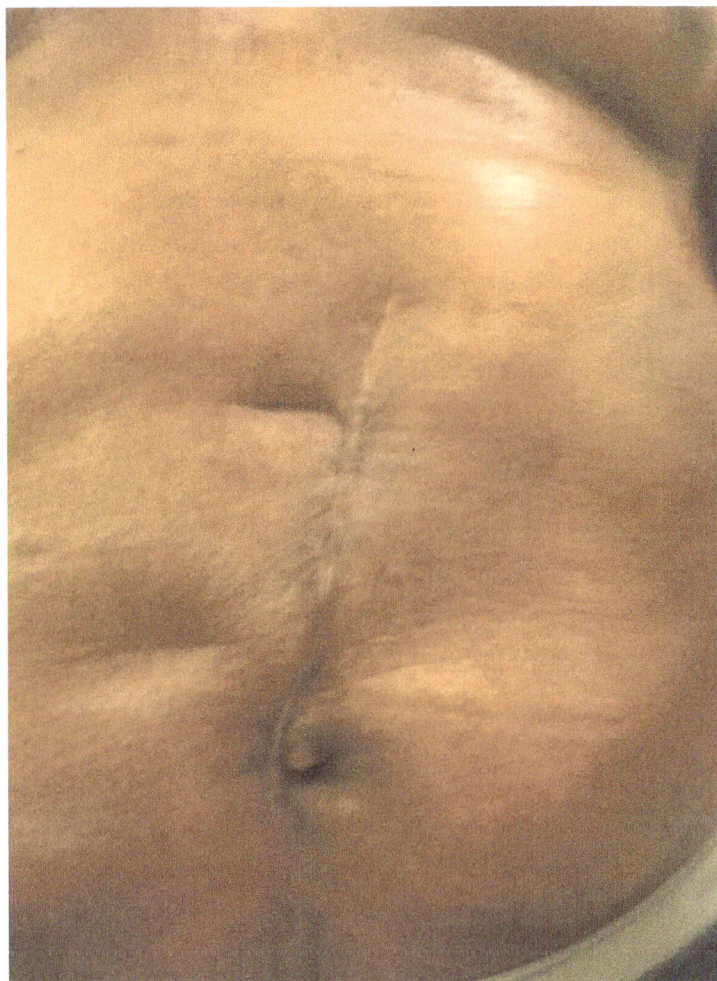

My scar after the left kidney was removed due to the cancer infection on it.

Encouragement

I have to say, I neglected my health. I ate poorly. Even after my doctors gave me the medicine, I did not take it. I have learned that there was more I could have done. My work was more important than my health. I know it sounds crazy but work was everything to me. I gained my sense of self-esteem and pride from what I did.

My focus and my mindset were all about work. I worked twelve to sixteen hour days. During my work hours, I did not eat properly and I did not get the proper amount of rest. On a typical day, I slept four to five hours a night.

But I had to work. Providing for my family was more important to me than my own health. While that seems noble, it is not safe. Even after transplant surgery, I wanted to get home so that I could get back to work. I know it sounds crazy but that was my mindset.

Over time, I realized that some of the health concerns and health challenges that I had, I brought it on myself because I neglected my health.

My advice to you is: Take care of yourself.

Do not neglect yourself. Do not put your health on the back burner. Listen to your body. Listen to your doctors. Work is not the most important thing…your life is.

Notes:

Chapter NINE

FOOT, BONE & LEG

Do you know what it feels like to be eaten alive?

I do. It literally feels like being pulled apart gradually, piece by agonizing piece. My flesh was slowly being eaten away by the disease. There was an increasing pain that surged through my foot. Sometimes the pain was so sharp it would make my eyes water. It was the type of pain you had to stop and shake off. Some moments the ache was so intense, I would physically shake my arms or head in the hopes to dislodge the stinging.

I never thought it could happen to me. I never imagined that my body would turn on itself. Like an internal suicide mission, one part of my body fought against the rest.

I felt the panic in the room. I watched as the doctors and nurses kept their backs turned to me to hide their faces. I struggled to hear the muted conversations between the team. I leaned in to understand what their hurried movements meant.

They didn't know how to tell me exactly what had happened. In the background, I heard the faint whispers of "osteomyelitis" and "bone infection." The whispers coupled with the grave concern in the room told me that I needed to brace myself.

I tried to steady myself in the chair. I held my hands together, almost in prayer. Anxiously, I switched my position by moving my feet further apart and holding the sides of the chair. I physically tried to brace myself for the weight of whatever the team of doctors would tell me.

I looked at the team. Then I looked at the floor. I looked at the machines. Then I looked at the floor again. I stared at the ceiling in a failed effort to pray but I was too afraid. I hardly spoke a word…the anticipation was killing me. Literally.

"Mr. Gray you have an infection in your bones. It is literally eating your foot from the inside out. The disease is aggressive and will move quickly. Therefore, we have to take an assertive approach to try and kill it", the doctor explained.

He stared at me for a moment as if to wait for my questions. I stared back at my doctor as if to telepathically send my thoughts to him. I didn't know what to ask. My only thought was…is this fatal? I didn't ask for fear that his response would be yes. I sat quietly with a secret hope that he would change his mind.

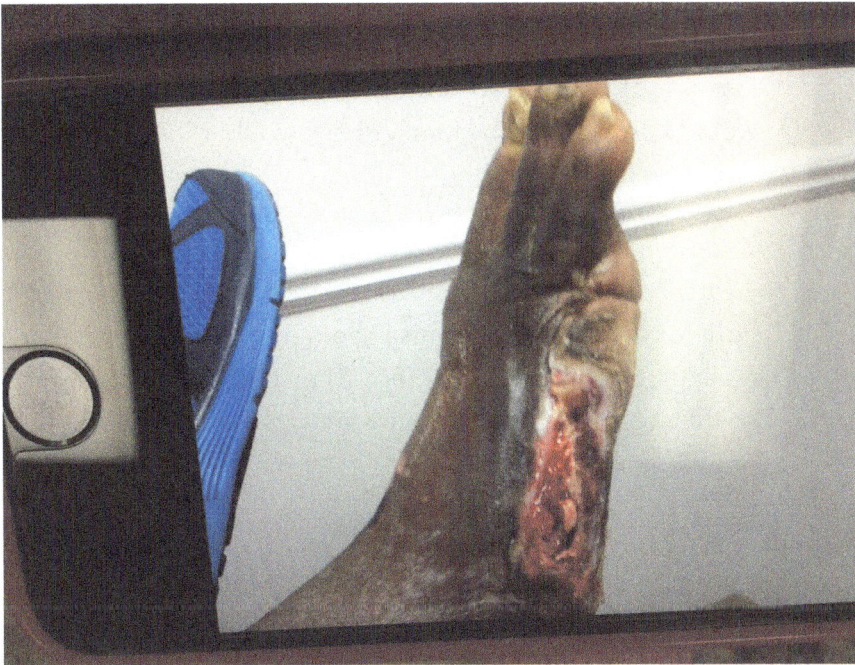

Fourth and fifth toe amputation and the effects of osteomyelitis

The aggressive approach was to amputate my foot. They said it was the most effective way to combat the disease. If they amputated the foot, it would prevent the spread of the flesh-eating bacteria.

"You can't take my foot!" I screamed.

Maybe I startled the doctors but I didn't care. To them, it was just a "foot" to me it was my life and my livelihood. How would I provide for my family? How would I walk? How would I be myself?

I watched the team's shock as I responded. I felt like I had to fight for my foot. No one else seemed to understand my feelings, but it wasn't their foot. They had both of their feet, so they couldn't get it. I was instantly defensive and on guard.

Another doctor from the team came to speak with me. His approach was even more radical. He felt they needed to take the leg just below the kneecap.

"You can't take my leg!" I screamed again.

At that moment, I didn't care about their professional opinion. All I knew was that I walked into the hospital and I planned to walk out the same way.

Literally, I could feel this slow moving pain travel up my foot. As I spoke to the medical team and waited for their response, I was in tremendous pain. I watched my foot closely and hoped that somehow this flesh eating disease would just stop. I hope against surgery. I believed just to be healed. However, I did not have the energy to question the doctor's decisions, so I just conceded.

Reluctantly, I went into surgery. The team amputated my fourth toe. A month later the doctors amputated my fifth toe and the third, fourth and fifth metatarsal bones on my right foot. I felt myself slowly move from defensive to depression.

Part of my recovery required that I go to a hyperbaric chamber for several weeks. The "medicine" in the hyperbaric chamber was pure oxygen. The oxygen directly poured on me for an hour or two every day. The doctors said the pure oxygen would increase my body's ability to recover.

It would be my first time experiencing one of these. My chamber was isolated in a separate part of the hospital. I could not have any visitors in the room at all. No one was even allowed into this area of the hospital. The chamber gave me more time to think and deal with the depression.

As I laid in this big, clear bubble, my thoughts taunted me. Would this work? Was this the final step before they amputated my entire foot? Or worse…amputate my entire leg?

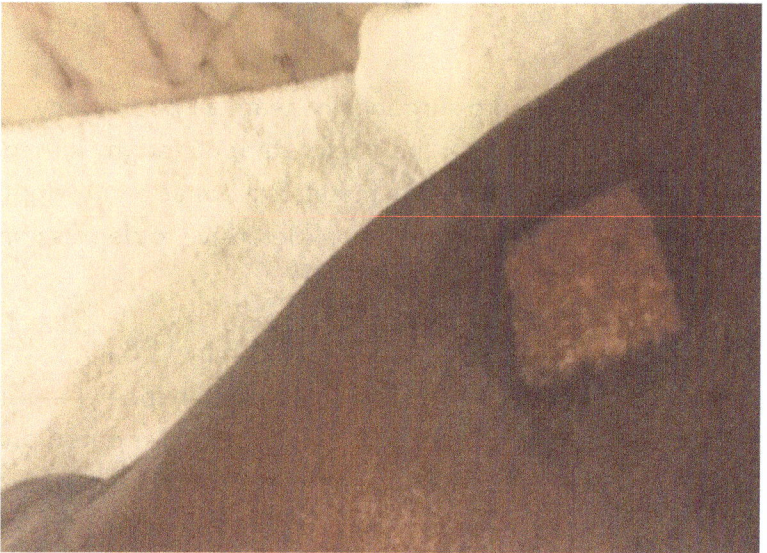

Skin graft from my upper thigh

(used for my foot)

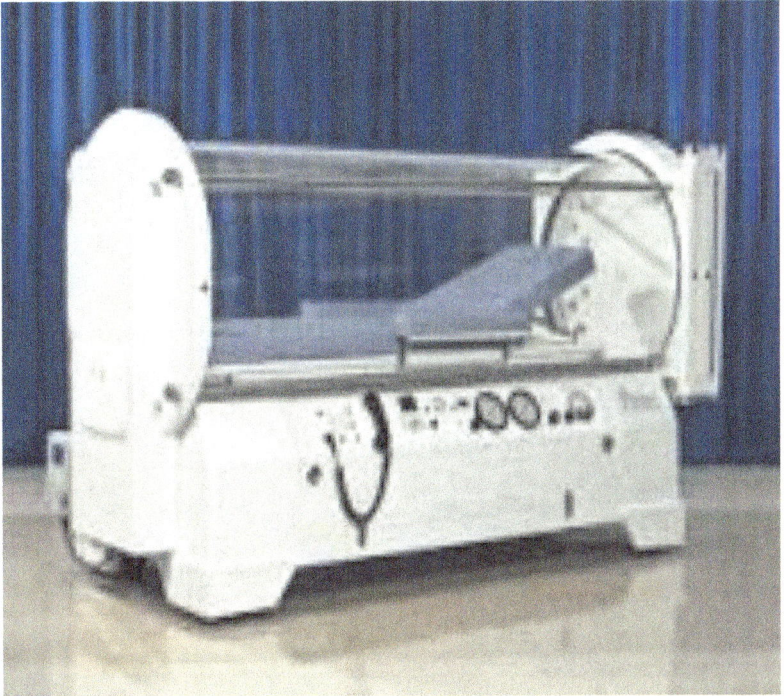

Hyperbaric chamber

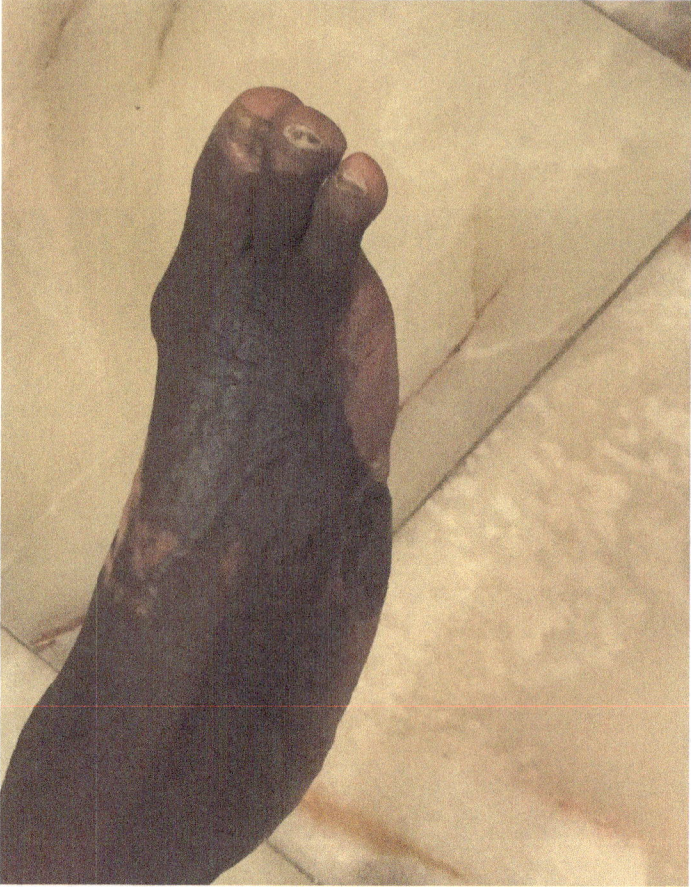

My healed foot

Encouragement

Lessons From A Caretaker

I would not have been able to make it through these past twenty years without my wife, Denise. She has been my caretaker. Her ability to stare in the face of my sickness and not blink (in fear) was life saving. The wisdom of God that she operated in was so critical to me, I asked her to share it with you.

Here are some of her lessons:

➢ Take care of the person with the love of God. His love is unconditional. Although it seems impossible, it is doable. Take care of the person the way you want to be treated and cared for.

➢ Be compassionate. Remember no one wants to be sick. If the roles were reversed, how would you like to be treated? Let's make sure that we treat each other in the same manner.

➢ Remember, they are sick. You are not. So be thankful for the strength to take care of them. Often times we take our health for granted. As the caregiver, your health is important. Always thank God for the strength He has given you…it is a blessing.

➢ Encourage them and pray for them. Being sick can take a toll on your mind as well as your body. Encouragement and prayer are essential tools that we can use to bless our loved ones. Use them often and consistently.

➢ Only allow strong, compassionate believers to visit. In other words, know it is ok to limit visitation. When Holloway was sick, I limited the people who would visit him. They had to be people of faith. They had to be people who would speak their faith over him when they saw him. They also had to be people who would be compassionate and not run in fear when they saw him.

➢ Don't get discouraged when people don't ask about you or how you are feeling. Your health matters but in that moment, the concern is often directed to the person you are taking care of.

In order to stay encouraged, continue in prayer and encourage yourself. You may not get much encouragement, so you will need to "encourage yourself in the Lord like David did." (1 Samuel 30:6)

➢ Lastly, take time to rejuvenate and pamper yourself. Your health and strength are critical. You need to be at your best, in order to serve them effectively.

Don't feel guilty for taking care of yourself. It's important. Think of things that rejuvenate you.

List them below:

1._____

2._____

3._____

4._____

5._____

6._____

7._____

8._____

9._____

10._____

So eat a cupcake, go to the spa, or get a massage. Enjoy a movie, a concert, whatever it takes for you to have some "me time". You deserve it.

Notes:

Chapter TEN

WHY AM I STILL HERE?

In June 2012, I went into the hospital to have tests run. Denise encouraged me to go because I wasn't feeling like myself and I was having trouble breathing. I went in for tests to see what was wrong. When my results came back, it showed that my creatinine levels were high and my blood had become infected. When your creatinine levels are elevated, it is a strong indication that your kidneys are not functioning correctly. My new transplanted kidneys had somehow become infected and they needed to be removed. I ended up having pneumonia and admitted in the ICU for 9 days. It quickly went from bad to worse.

I had a tube in my throat, a tube in my nose, pneumonia in both lungs, lost my set of transplanted kidneys, infected blood, a temperature of 104°, my pulse was over 100, and in a semi-comatose state. The nurses tied me to the bed so that I would not rip out the tubes in my throat.

I was attached to a hemodialysis machine due to the infection in my blood, a respirator to breathe for me, and a machine for my heart. The hemodialysis machine ran continuously. The doctors used it to help remove the infection in my blood. They also had to put me in a comatose state, to allow my body to rest and recover from the trauma that had happened.

My health went from bad to worse. I had several blood transfusions. The doctors had to shock my heart. My heartbeat was so irregular and would constantly flutter. The only way to stop the flutter was to jolt it. As scary as it sounded at the time, it was the easiest part of those 9 days.

I lost the use of my legs and my arms and I was unable to speak. If life is a fight, then I was losing. Somehow each day, I became worse. The devil tried to kill me and it looked like the curse had won.

I was in such bad condition that visitors had to wear a gown, mask and gloves to come into the room. This was to protect me from them. My immune system was so weak that the slightest change could literally make me worse.

I was dying.

Lots of people came to see me; their presence filled the waiting room. To be shown that much love was priceless. It was standing room only as coworkers, friends and family came to support me. Denise did not allow people into my room, only the closest people to our family were allowed in. Denise did not want anyone to bring in any fear or doubt. Only 'faith' was allowed into the room with us.

There was a constant rotation of doctors and nurses that moved in and out of my room. Every moment was intense and more critical than the moment before.

The 9 days in ICU, I was in and out of consciousness. I knew that my wife Denise, Gerald, Pastor Winfield, Pastor Robinson, and Bishop Jakes were there only because they told me after I left the hospital. I do not remember anything about those 9 days. I will let them tell you their thoughts about that time.

Pastor Winfield and I work together at our church. He is not just our colleague, his is our friend. He said

"There is an old phrase that we used to describe the worse possible outcome. Plain and simple, Holloway looked like life after death. He had tubes in his mouth and his eyes were closed for most of my visit. It was terrible to see him like that.

Despite what his body looked like, I was only concerned about his eyes. I waited to see if Holloway would open his eyes. After a while, I walked over to his bed and called his name. 'Holloway, if you can hear me, open your eyes,' and slowly he opened them.

As I looked at him, I asked one question; 'Are you going to fight this?' Although he could not speak, the look in his eyes showed his determination. There was a look in his eyes that said 'Hell yeah.' I knew he would make it because of the determination I saw he had."

Gerald has been our friend for over 25 years. Good, bad and ugly, he knows us. He said ...

"I knew when I got the phone call to come to the hospital from Denise that something was wrong. Denise never called over an issue; her calls were usually about church or family. Denise was never easily shaken but there was something different about her voice that made me drop everything to be with them.

If you know Holloway, you know he's real talkative and he's real loud. But that day in the hospital, he wasn't any of that. He was unresponsive and his body was limp. The only thing that could respond were his eyes. The old folks used to say he looked like death alive. That's how Holloway looked...like death, alive.

'Hey, Holloway, Gerald here.' After a few moments, he opened his eyes and stared at me. I didn't know if he was conscious or unconscious until he blinked his eyes. Then he slowly focused on me and I stared back at him into his eyes. His look told me he's gonna' give it his best shot. He still had fight left in him. He blinked and went back to sleep. It wasn't much but I knew he would do all he could to fight for his life."

His brother, Pastor Lawrence Robinson is another close family friend. We have known Lawrence for at least 25 years also. Lawrence saw me the following day. After he had spoken with Denise and Gerald, he left work to be by my side.

"If you know Holloway, you know he's a fighter. He's what we used to call hard to handle. He is full of life and he can't be tamed or stopped. Which is why I will never forget the day I saw him in the hospital.

I had been to the hospital many times with Holloway. I had seen him in good health and in bad, but that day was the worst I had ever seen him. I watched family members die, so

I am familiar with the 'death' look. And I am acutely familiar with the sound and smell of death but Holloway had it.

His skin was this ashy gray color. Every inch of his body was gray. His natural brown complexion was gone. He felt cold. His skin wasn't soft at all; it was just stiff and hard. He looked so bad; you didn't want to touch him. He didn't even look like himself.

I fought back tears when I looked at him. But instead of crying, I spoke to him like normal. 'Hey, man. Come on, you've got to pull through this. I know you're tired man but you've got to fight this. We need you. Denise needs you. Come on Holloway, FIGHT!'

I stared at him in the bed for another minute. I hoped that he would move, breathe, or do anything to let me know that he heard me, but there was nothing. He didn't move or make a sound. All I could do was trust that his spirit heard me.

'Come on Holloway, you've got to fight,' I thought as I slowly walked out of his room. I deliberately took off my protective suit, my mask, my gloves and cap like I was removing the image off of me. It seemed like a horrible nightmare until I looked back through the glass of his room door only to be reminded this was no dream.

My friend was dying and all I could do was watch and pray."

Bishop Jakes is not only my Pastor he is my friend. He came to visit me while I was in ICU these 9 days. Denise recalls this particular visit with him when he came very clearly.

"Throughout Holloways process and sickness overall and when needed to know, Bishop was informed of Holloway's health disparities. In this instance, however, I kept Bishop aware and up to date of his condition directly. Holloway's situation was critical. It concerned me, it concerned us all, but it didn't shake me. Bishop called and told me he was going to come by and see him. When he came, he wanted to know how I was holding up; I told him that I was good. I knew what God's Word said and what He showed me and I believed Him and I am standing on His promises.

I told Bishop that he had to wear the special clothing, mask and garments before he could go in and see Holloway. I stopped him before he walked in and said, 'brace yourself, Bishop, he looks real bad. You have never seen him like this before.'

Bishop had a concerned look on his face as he put on the mask. But he turned around and walked in like a warrior. I left them alone so he could talk with his friend privately. When

Bishop came out of that room, he said, "He looks like he is at the portals of eternities gate!" He was concerned, but not fearful. He and I both knew that no matter how he looked, he was going to come out of this. His faith matched mine along with everyone else's and we fought to stand on God's Word.

When Bishop left, he called on all the saints to pray. He notified everyone that would hear him, and he called on the intercessors to reach the thrones of heaven. People began to pray all over the world for Holloway. He was knocking on the doors to infinity, but God heard us. He heard our cry and our hearts, and He closed the portals to eternity for now.

And Holloway got up.

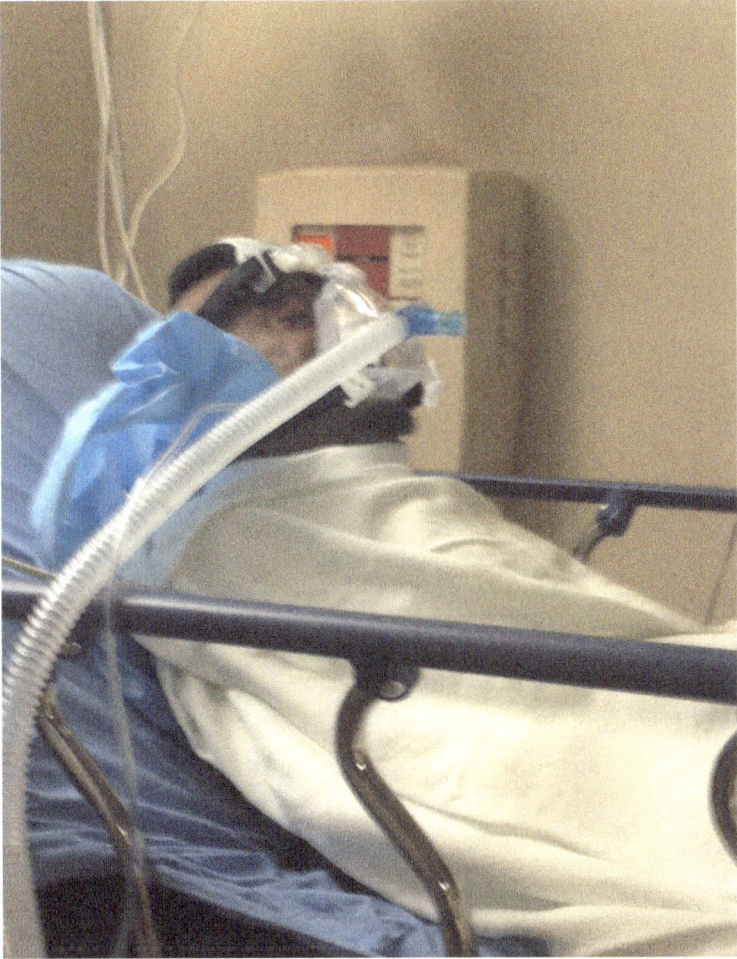

9 days on the ventilator machine in the ICU unit, fighting for my life. I went in weighing 220lbs and came out weighing 165lbs.

Encouragement

Hang Your Plaque.

During these 9 days, we were in the fight of our lives. Looking back at this time there were so many lessons we learned. We were standing on our faith and our belief in GOD. Sometimes our faith and creed look foolish to others but even when it looks senseless, do it anyway.

While I was in the ICU, my wife, Denise did something that probably seemed foolish. Denise hung a plaque over my bed. The plaque stated what we believed and it said simply this: "This family believes in long life, miracles, love, and faith." She made sure it was placed on the dresser so whoever entered the room would see it, read it, and confess it. She believed it 100% and didn't want anyone coming in my room that didn't feel the same way.

With tubes in my body, and machines that encircled my bed, Denise still declared her faith. It looked ridiculous to hang a plaque over (what some would consider a death bed). But she did it anyway. She did not see me on a deathbed. She saw me alive and well.

Denise wanted to make sure that every doctor and nurse knew what we believed. Every person that walked into my room was informed of our belief system and what outcome we expected. It changed the feeling in there. That plaque helped to keep all of us focused.

With that said, I have one piece of advice. While you are waiting for the victory...hang your plaque.

Notes:

_____

_____

_____

_____

_____

_____

_____

_____

_____

_____

_____

_____

_____

_____

_____

_____

_____

_____

_____

_____

_____

_____

_____

_____

_____

_____

Chapter ELEVEN

THE CURSE IS BROKEN

July 6, 2014. Church Anniversary.

That Sunday started off like most Sundays. We had to get ready for church. Denise grabbed a pretty peach dress that I loved seeing her in. I grabbed my black pants and red blazer. But I didn't grab it too hard because I couldn't move as fast. It takes me much longer to get dressed than Denise.

Due to my foot surgeries, I could only wear one shoe while my other foot was in a boot. I debated for several minutes on which tie to wear but I decided to choose the darker of the two. I liked to look my best at church.

Since I work and volunteer at our church, our day begins early. Denise made my usual breakfast, bacon, eggs, toast and oatmeal but because of the time, we quickly grabbed our juice for the car drive. As usual, we listened to our favorite gospel station in the car ride there. And I appreciate the ride because it gives me time to use my "other" talent. I can sing you know. I am not sure that Denise would agree but she listens to me anyway. It's something about the acoustics in the car and the gospel music as my background that makes me scream the words at the top of my lungs. Regardless of the gospel song, most Sunday morning drives you will find me driving and singing (screaming) the lyrics.

I walked into church like I do every Sunday morning, dressed with a smile. I answered a few questions and greeted a few people. I clutched my Bible tightly in my right hand as I walked into the sanctuary. I was prepared for a rooted word.

We sat in our usual spot, in the front right-hand side closest to the stage. As I sat in my seat, I asked God a question. I asked Him how could I promote my book? The answer to my question was right in front of me. At the same time, Bishop Jakes mentioned me. "This guy right here," he started off as he motioned to me, "developed the foundation for the church move from West Virginia to Dallas, TX."

I was so humbled that Bishop Jakes mentioned me and my role in the church move. It was an experience that I have treasured since I was given the opportunity. In that moment I was thankful to God for entrusting such a responsibility to me.

As the service continued, I leaned forward in my seat as if Bishop was about to tell me a secret. And as a child of God, I knew His voice and I expected to hear it every Sunday. And without fail, every Sunday, God spoke through my Pastor to me.

While Bishop Jakes spoke that day in church, God spoke to me. It never ceased to amaze me that the same God who controls the universe had time to speak to me. God said, "You have suffered with Me and now you will reign with Me." I immediately knew that the curse was broken. Then He said, "The sky is the limit."

When I heard these words, my spirit leaped. God's timing was perfect. It was the exact moment when I needed to hear from Him. Down in my soul, I knew my struggle was finished….***the curse was broken***. I just knew that I did not have to worry about it anymore.

The physical manifestation of my healing did not take place as I sat in my seat. However, I knew beyond a shadow of a doubt that the struggle was over and I had won!

After the service, I felt the same peace of mind that I had earlier in the service. There was an ease and relief in my soul after I heard from the Holy Spirit.

Days later in my usual routine, I went outside on my way to the car and I simply looked up to the sky. It reminded me of the ocean; there is no end to it. There is no end to the sky. Then it dawned on me; the blessing will be eternal. It will go on forever and ever and there will not be an end to it.

That realization changed by expectation. I fully expected a tremendous harvest for all the torment and torture I had been through. I believed God was going to bless me in order to bless others.

It took a lot of prayers; it took a lot of strength and stability. I am still amazed and most grateful that GOD would give me the victory.

July 6, 2014.

The day the curse was broken.

"You have suffered with Me, now you will reign with Me. The sky is the limit."

Encouragement

I want to remind you that GOD has the final say. Even when you feel like you are hanging on by a thread, GOD has the last word. He is not afraid of the situation. He has all power.

I also want to remind you that God's timing is perfect. He is never late. He is always perfectly on time. I know that it seems like things have gone from bad to worse. Let me remind you what Galatians 6:9 says: "Do not get weary in well doing for in the proper time you will reap if ye faint not."

We just have to decide what we believe:

Do we believe that the situation is bigger than our GOD?

Or

Do we believe nothing is greater than our GOD? Do we believe things have gone from bad to worse?

Or

Do we believe that nothing is impossible to them who believe?

We have to decide what we believe and whether or not we want the victory.

Do you want the victory?

If you want the victory, you can have it! Make a decision despite what you are going through; you will be victorious. I am going tell you it may be hard and it may be difficult. I went through challenges, situations and life-threatening health issues. I went through pain and I went through agony. I went through suffering and I went through torment.

Guess what? I've got the victory. I have decided I want to continue in the win. Now, in order to keep being successful daily, I choose to live and walk in the fullness of God.

Now, it's up to you. Answer these questions as you decide:

1. What do you want to do?
2. Do you want the victory?

Notes:

Chapter TWELVE

THE LAST WORD

The more I looked at the deaths that occurred in my family, the clearer the curse became. The curses in our family were: premature death, death from diabetes, hypertension, kidney disease, and sudden death from heart attacks. Many members of my family were destroyed prematurely because of the curse. As scary as these events were, I had to stand up to them and identify them as such.

To this day, I do not know how far back the curse goes. However, I know this evil will not go beyond me. My family will no longer be plagued by it.

I am often asked how I broke the curse. Well, I didn't break the curse…God did. However, there is a part that I played. It took 10 years of sacrifice, suffering and near death experiences, but GOD delivered me.

During the sickness, I did not fast because I am a diabetic and I take medication that requires me to eat food. However, I prayed. My family prayed. Our entire church prayed. I believe prayer is one of strongest tools we have.

Our pastor, Bishop T.D. Jakes sent out an S.O.S. for me. We requested everyone that could pray, should pray for my healing. And they did. Our church family prayed. I could feel all the prayers surrounding me. No matter my condition or how I felt at the moment, I knew that I had the camaraderie and the support of the saints. Those prayers were powerful and effective in my life.

I studied the scriptures. There was not just one that I read and stood on. I just read the Word. Sometimes just a verse or a word would say so much to me and as I read it, it always encouraged me.

I listened to the Word as much as I could. Whenever it was being taught, I was there. Whatever was being taught, I listened to it. Whoever taught it, I received it as a direct Word from God to me.

I remembered the promises of God. Many things have been promised to us but have we taken the time to research the promises for ourselves? Honestly, I took many of the promises of GOD for granted. It was not until I cried out to Him in a drug fog that I began to search for the promises myself. I needed God desperately and He rescued me.

One vow that I stood on constantly was for long life. Our Father promises us that if we would honor our father and mother that our days would be long on the earth. (Ephesians 6:1 "Children obey your parents in the Lord for this is right. That it may go well with you and that you may live long in the land"). This is the first commandment with a promise.

I learned this scripture as a child and because of my upbringing; it was easy to honor my parents. I knew that regardless of my condition, I was eligible for this promise.

The one thing I did more than anything was to keep it moving. In other words, I kept my focus on my recovery. Mentally, I never stopped in the middle of my sickness. I never stopped in the middle of my depression. I kept it moving as much as possible.

Whenever I could get back to work, I worked. Whenever I could get back to serve, I served. If I could work and help, then I was in my element. Sometimes you have to do what is best for you. In my case, that was service and work. It caused me to survive. I went into the lion's den for myself, by myself. Most times I felt like it was only me and God.

Everyone around me told me to slow down. However, I didn't pay them any attention, but I did appreciate all of their prayers and support. I could feel the love and genuine concern of the saints, which fueled my tenacity all the more. Their support enabled me to fight.

No matter how sick you become, keep it moving. No matter how confused you become, keep it moving. No matter how depressed you become, keep it moving. No matter how bad it gets, keep it moving.

Do the things or tasks that you used to do before you got sick. Do the things or tasks you used to do before the tragedy hit. Practice walking and working in your own recovery. You will win if you don't quit. Please hear me when I say, You Will Win! The next step could get you the victory.

I am grateful that I never stopped in the middle of my sickness. Never stopped in the middle of my depression. I have been through many levels of depression during the state of my illness but I never stopped.

I had to fight the curse. I stood up to the curse to break it. What I mean is that no matter what came my way, I faced it and I did not back down. I would not quit. I would not hide from the sickness. I confronted it!

I believe that if we stand up, God will stand up with us. I stood up and God stood with me. Literally, my faith has increased. I don't know how many more levels it will grow, but know that my faith is stronger.

Each time I stood against my sickness, I got stronger. Each time I stood against my sickness, I had the victory. Each time I stood against my sickness, my faith was enhanced and my roots were planted deeper. My tree may have bent under the pressure but the devil never broke me. I stood up!

There was tenacity in me who some would call meanness, that would not let me die. That tough streak in me kept me living. Without it, I would have been dead. It gave me the tenacity to live. It gave me the push to keep fighting. For whatever reason, I was mad enough to say, I will not die. I will not give up. I will not break. I will stand up.

No matter what happens in your life, stand up to it. Life is unfair. Life is hard. Don't cry about it. Stand up to it. Stand up to life.

When I was sick, I could have complained, murmured or even quit. Even in the lowest stages of my depression, this tenacity made me want to live. I believed there was a purpose and I believed that God would show His power and strength.

The reality is you have to stand up to life. Stand up. Life will destroy you if you don't get up. As sick I was, I realized that I didn't have anything else to lose. I could not run from it either.

You can't escape from your sickness. You can't run from your pain. You can't hide from the tragedy. You have to stand up to it. The only way to win is to face it square in the eyes.

The first time you stand up, you overcome. The second time you stand up, it becomes easier. The third time you stand up, it becomes better. The fourth time you stand up, you have now tapped into greatness.

You can do it!

You can beat this!

Stand up!

Final

Encouragement

Even now as I write this book, I am in the midst of a battle. My body has once again been attacked. The devil has fought me on every hand to prevent this book from being completed. From the death of my mother, the effects of grief and apathy, and more sickness, the attack has been both mental and physical.

I know this challenge will bring out the change. I know this fight is not with anyone but the enemy and me. The obstacles that are in my way will have to move. I have decided I will not back up off my faith and I will not give up. The victory is already mine. I am still standing.

I have been blessed with prayer warriors that have taken me under their wing to pray for me and to pray with me. I am grateful that God has given me and given us this weapon of prayer.

We pray in the morning, afternoon and evening to stop the enemy. I need the daily communion with God. This season has strengthened my faith and my relationship with Him. I know His Word is working for me.

I take communion two times a day. Also, I anoint my body with oil. I believe this will stop the enemy. I know that God has used all of this in my life for His good and allowed me to see His glory in it. I believe there is something great behind this battle.

I hope that my story has enlightened you and caused you to look at your own family. I hope that everything I have fought through has encouraged you. I hope that my life has been a testament to you of the faithfulness of God. If He has been faithful to me, He will be faithful to you.

I do not mind showing you my scars. They prove to you that I have been in a battle. The fact that I am here to tell you about this war only shows you that I have been victorious.

The same victory that I have experienced is the same victory I want you to have.

- ➤ Never give up!
- ➤ Fight the good fight!
- ➤ Live victoriously.

Notes:

172

CPSIA information can be obtained
at www.ICGtesting.com
Printed in the USA
FSOW03n1750290416
19884FS

9 780981 751054